DARK PSYCHOLOGY 101

Learn Five Secret Techniques of Forbidden Manipulation for Limitless Mind Control Using the Art of Neuro-linguistic Programming for Social Influence and Persuasion

By Jack Hill

Disclaimer

The content of this book has been checked and compiled with great care. For the completeness, correctness and topicality of the contents however no guarantees can be made. The content of this book represents the personal experience and opinion of the author and is for entertainment purposes only. The content should not be confused with medical help. There will be no legal responsibility or liability for damages resulting from counterproductive exercise or errors by the reader. No guarantee can be given for success. The author, therefore, assumes no responsibility for the non-achievement of the goals described in the book.

Table of Contents

INTRODUCTION

Is There Such Thing As Mind Control Or Manipulation?

Many people are asking themselves: is there such a thing as mind control? There are movies made about it, there are novels which use thought control stories, there are sometimes articles in magazines and newspapers. But does this psychological technology really exist, or is it just a myth?

First of all, it should be mentioned that mind control both exists and doesn't exist. It's simply a matter of how you define it. If you think of it as some kind of machine that you can attach another person's brain to, and then the machine somehow reprograms their mind and is essentially some kind of total brainwashing, then the answer is: no, this does not exist outside of comic books.

However, there are more subtle ways of bending minds, that are nonetheless dangerously effective if used by the wrong people.

In fact, mind control is nothing else than highly effective persuasion. Think of it this way: if persuasion is a flashlight, then thought control is a laser beam. Both the light ray of a flashlight and a laser beam are "just light", but the effects they have are very different. You can do things with lasers that you could never do with a flashlight.

Mind control is often a form of very systematically layered persuasion. For example, peer group pressure surely doesn't feel like thought control, after all, it is something that even teenagers instinctively make use of. Yet, combined with other persuasive elements, it can be used for manipulative psychological purposes.

Mind control is being used by political interest parties and large organizations, as well as religious sects and cults, by individuals to influence others and in one-to-one communication situations. Social influence techniques are used to alter the environment of a person to change the way they think and change what they think about. Oftentimes, a person is being isolated from his or her previous social environment, so that more influence can be exerted over him or her. There is typically also a very purposeful destruction of a person's sense of self, his or her reality and values that takes place.

If you think of the terrorist attacks of 9/11 - the people who have been involved in carrying out these attacks have been under the influence of mind control. They were intelligent people, yet, somehow dark powers persuaded them into believing that killing thousands of innocent people would be something their god would approve of. While this is an extreme example of thought control, be aware that to some extent, we are all under the influence of mind control, and the better we understand the mechanisms of mental control, the more we are able to protect ourselves from it.

THE 5 SECRET TECHNIqUES OF MANIPULATION

Manipulation is an act that implies abuse of power because it involves using discursive elements to control the cognition, affections, and behavior of one or more people. It is often confused or mixed with other similar processes: argumentation and persuasion, but they are not the same.

In this book, I will explain what manipulation is and how it differs from persuasion and argumentation. This book will also present some examples of manipulation techniques that are frequently used.

Argue, persuade and manipulate are not the same

Both argumentation and persuasion and manipulation can take the form of oral or written discourse and in very general terms serve to defend an idea or an attitude, so it is very easy to confuse them. What makes them different is the purpose pursued by each, as well as its particular elements.

Argumentation is an activity that consists of giving logic and coherence to an idea to defend it. In other words, it is when we establish reasoning with a specific purpose: to justify or refute that or other reasoning.

On the other hand, persuasion occurs when the argument has a further purpose: it is not only used to defend or refute an idea but is aimed at modifying the behavior of the interlocutor.

Also, manipulation is when the argument is used to modify or direct the behavior of the interlocutor, but based on two main elements and purposes: power, or rather the abuse of power, which translates into domination.

It can be very subtle (it usually goes unnoticed) and can constitute the foundations of symbolic violence since it has the result of favoring the interests of one party and damaging those of the other.

That is why manipulation can be analyzed from three dimensions (Van Dijk, 2006): a social one, which is exercised by elites who have access to public discourse, so their influence is on a large scale; a cognitive dimension that consists of controlling mental models and social representations; and a discursive dimension, which consists of using linguistic elements to be able to impact both the mental schemas and the behaviors of a person or of a whole group.

Some manipulation techniques

Studies on how some groups or individuals manipulate others have become very frequent in recent decades, especially in the area of media, advertising, and political activity.

Thanks to this we have been able to identify some manipulation strategies in which we can fall for very easily without realizing it, both in our interpersonal relationships and in what we see daily on television or the Internet.

Although I could exemplify many more, I will review 5 of the most common manipulation techniques.

1. Play with feelings and emotions

Controlling the affective dimension is one of the most powerful tools because it makes the receptors reaffirm their opinions and positions without necessarily having gone through logical, reflective or critical reasoning.

An example could be the activity of the tabloid press, which exaggerates the news by giving information a touch of sensationalism rather than rigor, because the objective is precisely to appeal to the emotional dimension of the readers and their previous experiences, and With this, increase visits or sales.

2. Simplify the message and include strong affirmations

It consists of controlling the cognitive elements that

allow us to process and understand a message. It is when quick and strong conjectures are used that they do not give the possibility of deep analysis, which is basically to intentionally obstruct the understanding of the argument.

For example, when a small part of a text is printed in large, underlined letters and at the beginning, which in addition to immediately attracting our attention and activating short-term memory, causes us to have a partial or biased understanding of the information.

3. To resort to what authority says or thinks

It is when a position is justified by presenting a person or a figure that is socially recognized as a competent authority. This is useful because we often tend to consider more the opinions, indications or activities of someone we admire or someone who is in a position of power.

This can imply from the opinion of a priest or a president to that of an artist or a relative, and its effectiveness depends on the context in which the group or person develops.

4. Identify conflicts and make them think that they are always the same

It is when a situation, especially if it is a conflictive

situation, is reduced to what a single person or group of people do, say or think, hiding all the other variables, agents or groups that also influence or are affected by that situation, contributing to a generalization of knowledge, affect, attitude or ideology .

An example is found in the cases that occur when an attack is represented in the mass media as an isolated event, or as the act of a "madman" (with which we are invited to fear all those who seem), instead of being represented as the result of complex political and social conflicts.

5. Use and reinforce stereotypes

Very roughly, stereotypes are the behavioral qualities that are attributed in a simplified and almost automatic way to a person or a group of people.

This is a useful persuasion technique because it allows you to control values and judgments without having to justify the arguments deeply and without allowing the receiver to question themselves.

WHAT IS DARK PSYCHOLOGY?

Dark Psychology is the study of both manipulation and mind control of the human mind. While Psychology is the study of human behavior and is hinged majorly on our actions, thoughts and interactions, the name Dark Psychology, as stated, is referred to as the system in which individuals, both young and old, use schemes of persuasion, motivation, manipulation and even compulsion to acquire what they want.

Dark Psychology Triad

Both the history of the world and everyday life are filled with examples of people acting ruthlessly, maliciously or selfishly.

In psychology, as in everyday language, we have several names for the various dark tendencies that the human being may have, among which are psychopathy (lack of empathy), narcissism (excessive self-absorption), and Machiavellianism (the belief that ends justify the means).

Specifically, these three traits form what psychologists

13

call the "triad of darkness," to which many others join, such as selfishness, sadism, or wickedness.

What has now been discovered is that these "black side" traits seem to share a common dark core: anyone who has one of these tendencies is more likely to have one or more of the others.

Although at first glance there appear to be striking differences between these traits - or it may seem more "acceptable" to be selfish than a psychopath, for example - new research shows that all the dark aspects of human personality are closely linked and are based on the same trend.

Factor D

The common denominator of all dark traces was called the "D-factor," from the English word 'dark', which means gloomy or evil.

The D factor was defined by Morten Moshagen and his colleagues as the general tendency to maximize one's individual usefulness while at the same time disregarding, accepting, or maliciously provoking disutility for others, all accompanied by beliefs that serve as justifications for the acts themselves.

In other words, all the dark traits can be traced back to the general tendency of putting one's own goals and interests on those of others, to the point of feeling pleasure in hurting others - along with a series of beliefs that serve as justifications, thus avoiding feelings of guilt, shame or the like.

Research has shown that dark traits, in general, can be understood as instances of this common core, although they may differ in which aspects are predominant. For example, the aspect of the justifications is very strong in narcissism, while the aspect of provoking malevolent disutility is the main characteristic of sadism.

Dark personality traits

Moshagen and his colleagues demonstrated how this common denominator is present in nine of the most commonly studied dark personality traits:

- Selfishness: an excessive preoccupation with one's own advantage at the expense of others and the community.
- Machiavellianism: a manipulative and insensitive attitude and a belief that ends justify the means.
- Moral disengagement: a style of cognitive processing that allows one to behave in an unethical way without feeling anguish.
- Narcissism: excessive self-absorption, sense of superiority and extreme need for attention of others.

- Psychological law: a recurring belief of being better than others and deserving better treatment.
- Psychopathy: lack of empathy and self-control, combined with impulsive behavior.
- Sadism: A desire to inflict mental or physical harm on others for pleasure or benefit.
- Self-interest: desire to promote and highlight one's own social and financial status.
- Desire for revenge: destructiveness and willingness to harm others, even if someone harms you in the process.

Factor D indicates the likelihood of a person engaging in behavior associated with one or more of the dark personality traits.

"For example, in a given person, factor D may manifest primarily as narcissism, psychopathy or one of the other gloomy traits, or a combination of these.but with our mapping of the common denominator of the various traits of the somber personality, if you simply check that the person has a high D-factor, because D-factor indicates a person's likelihood of engaging in behavior associated with one or more of these dark traits, "said Moshagen.

In practice, this means that an individual who has a certain malevolent behavior (such as liking to humiliate others) is more likely to engage in other malicious activities.

Common elements of evil

The nine dark traits in no way generate the same results, and each can result in specific types of behavior. However, in essence, dark traits usually have much more in common than elements that differentiate them.

Knowledge about this "dark core" of personality can play a crucial role for researchers and therapists working with people with specific traits of shady personality since this D factor affects different types of reckless and malicious behavior and human actions often reported by media, the team says.

THE HISTORY
OF PERSUASION

To persuade is not to impose or deceive (differs from "imposition", "submission" or "deception")

The origin of persuasion goes back to ancient Greece: there the philosophers began to talk about something they called "rhetoric", conceived as the art of persuading or convincing through the special use of language, that is, using mental images, images (unsurpassable example to refer to something, such as the desert in relation to sterility, or death as the end of something, or the sky as a sign of purity) built on the basis of omissions or exaggerations, conceptual similarities between images (the sun as a substitution for a gold coin, for example), or using only a part of something to mention the whole ("bronzes" to mean bell).

All these communication techniques presuppose a certain effort both in the construction and in the decoding, but just the time of interpretation to which the brain is subjected to find the final idea, that construction work of the communicated concept, is what is called "rhetoric".

To speak with precision, in graphic design and in

advertising appeal to rhetoric given that it is known that the more interesting this reconstruction is by the brain, the clearer and longer the communicated concept will remain in it. Hence, the people of the field are called "creative", because they must create, rather, generate a mini-story, a journey between concepts, to finally give a closure that makes the message communicated more powerful for the mind.

It must be understood that persuasion is measured from the receiver and the degree of conviction generated in it. The convincing, then, is measured by the amount and direction of the thoughts generated in the receiver as a result of the information received. And, according to the "marketers" of today, it is virtually impossible to sell a service or without announcing it in some persuasive way today.

The object is then to generate a positive attitude in the receiver, and modify their attitude or generate an attitude of approach to the idea communicated. Historically, the great persuasive is Satan himself: in the form of a serpent, he convinces Adam and Eve to eat the apple that will make them aware of "good and evil". Good marketing technique, because the publicity he made did not refer to the taste.

Covert Persuasion Techniques That Will Change Your Life and Influence Others

Have you ever had the challenge of trying to negotiate or argue with an extremely stubborn person who resisted every offered compromise or solution? If so, then you probably already know that there are some people who do everything they can to avoid giving in to the wishes and persuasion of others. If you find yourself locked in a conflict with a person who resists common techniques of compromise and resolution, you might have to take your game to the next level and use covert persuasion.

Covert persuasion techniques work on a subconscious level to win over even the most stubborn, resistant people to your side. Even people who might never be open to your argument, product, or romantic advances in their conscious minds can often be influenced by using advanced covert persuasion techniques.

However, the skillful use of covert persuasion techniques is an art form that must be developed with careful practice and the guidance of a proven expert. If deployed improperly, you will wind up wasting your time - and potentially alienating the very person that you are trying to win over.

Even if you are trapped in a situation that seems doomed to end in a stalemate or another outcome that is undesirable to you, you can help turn things around with the use of covert persuasion techniques. Just be sure to learn everything you can about these sophisticated persuasion tools before you try to deploy them!

Facts About the Art of Persuasion

Many people think of persuasion as evil. Well, we're going to disprove this misconception right now because there is absolutely no truth in this common belief. Persuasion, more than anything, is a form of human communication. Persuasion is a sub-type of human communication that aims to introduce change in people. Of course, this is usually done to help manifest an ideal outcome for the speaker.

The art of persuasion can be applied to a variety of situations, from regular conversations to important meetings. Persuasion is used by politicians, marketers, advertisers, and even by your tough teachers back in high school. Persuasion, unlike power, has the capacity to reach out and introduce new concepts and ideas to a wide array of people without the need to resort to threats or punishment.

And unlike people who abuse authority or power, persuasive individuals are viewed as positive members of organizations and groups. The art of persuasion is used in political propaganda, speeches, television commercials, radio commercials, print advertising, etc.

Everywhere you look, strategies of persuasion are being used by businesses and organizations to fortify their respective positions and to stay on top of their game.

And now you too can enjoy the benefits of being truly persuasive. With this book, you can learn the basics of persuasion and how you can apply it to real-life situations. Just remember: persuasion is a skill, just like driving or skiing. You need to practice frequently to perfect it!

Why Emotions Matter in Persuasion

The classical approach to persuasion is to create elaborate arguments that will convince the other person to comply with whatever you're saying. Persuasion is mostly one-sided if we use this technique, and it won't work. People are no longer interested in traditional sales pitches, negotiations, etc. So what will work nowadays?

Based on the current literature on persuasion, the best way to persuade someone to believe in what you're saying is to tap into known emotional triggers. Emotions actually play a huge role in persuasion because people usually act based on their emotions. People rarely use their critical faculties once a persuader can tap into emotional triggers.

The most common emotional response is the buying response. If you watch television commercials close enough, you'll start to see triggers embedded in the commercials that prompt the audience to buy the advertised product. The triggers are subtle and yet, after days and weeks, it's possible for a person to suddenly want to buy that product - based on the memory of emotion that they felt while watching the television commercial.

So the next time you want people to agree with you, don't focus too much on facts and figures. Instead, try to appeal to your audience's emotions. Do this and you automatically have the upper hand. They'll become more trusting and they'll be more comfortable accepting your ideas.

Do Rewards Work?

Another classical method in the world of persuasion is the reward and punishment technique. I admit that this technique has its benefits. If you've ever seen an online sales letter (or a landing page), you know what I mean. These sales letters frequently make use of the reward and punishment model of persuasion.

If people agree with the arguments, they instantly get a chance to get the rewards. But if they disagree, people are 'punished' because their problems remain, they won't save money in the long-term, etc.

This model of persuasion might work in the short-term, but if you're a business owner and you want repeat business, you have to rethink your persuasive strategy. Even if this model worked in the beginning, people will eventually want more rewards because they're sticking with your business.

If you run out of concessions for your customers, they'll lose interest in your offers and will look for better offers. This fickle nature of consumers is the main reason why you should not depend wholly on the reward and punishment model. It's extremely tiring to keep giving concessions over a long time. Besides, this persuasion technique rarely creates a long-term impact on people, and that's what we want.

Many other strategies can create a big impact on your audience. You can appeal to your audience's intelligence (tell them that smart people choose your services and products), or you can tell them that over the long-term, they'll save a lot of money by choosing your idea or product.

Mastering the Art of Persuasion and Negotiation

There's no doubt that the skills of persuasion and negotiation are essential to anyone who wants to succeed in life. This is especially important if you have a message that you know has the power to change the world and help people to live better lives.

However, what a waste it would be if the world never heard your message because you didn't keep quiet long enough to listen and to understand what people really needed. If you like the sound of this, keep reading and find out why shutting up and listening can be the most powerful persuasion skill you'll ever learn.

Why You Should Aim to Master the Art of Persuasion

Think of the most persuasive person you know. It may be a doctor, a minister, a friend, a talk show host, a celebrity, etc. Perhaps you've wondered why some people have it and others don't. Those who stand out from the crowd and have the ease of persuasion have mastered certain skills that anyone can easily learn. Being persuasive to the point that moves another person to take a specific desired action is essential to any business and requires more than smooth words and a proven business system. And, wouldn't it be great if your prospects, clients, and customers didn't analyze every single word out of your mouth? Do you visualize your prospects believing what you say and doing business with you with ease of mind? Well, it's easier than you think with these 3 magic ingredients:

• **TRUST** - Just think of a relationship in your life where there is a high level of trust. How hard do you have to work to get the other person to listen, understand and to take you seriously? Trust is the one element that will either make or break your ability to persuade a person. You can be the most silver-tongued communicator that ever lived, but if the ability to build trust with your listener is lacking, you are going to encounter a serious roadblock to initiating any desired action from them. So what is the missing link which empowers you to build trust with someone faster than anything else?

• **UNDERSTANDING** - How can anyone be understanding without first listening? Listening can only take place if your prospect is engaged and talking... telling you their needs, desires, and asking questions. People feel comfortable when they have the opportunity to say what's on their mind, everyone wants to be heard. So, actively listening is the foundation of being persuasive. It is more than a notion that we have two ears and one mouth and that we should listen more than we speak. Most influential people say very few words but speak volumes. After you have successfully built trust and understanding through listening intently and thoughtful engagement, this final ingredient will cause the shift to persuasion, and without it, your prospect will not move toward the action that you desire them to take; so what is it?

• **COMPETENCE** - It's no secret that you really do have to know what you are talking about to influence others especially if it involves money, religion, sports or politics. Delivering a reasonable presentation based on solid usable information is critical to your success. Your prospect needs to have a reason to listen to you and more importantly, a reason to want to allow you to influence them. Part of competence involves building a relationship based on VALUE. If your prospect detects that you are knowledgeable, experienced and competent... capable and willing to help them achieve certain results, you will most likely score big in the persuasion department.

Attempting to advise or lead without understanding and/or building trust is a recipe for disaster. In fact, failure to build rapport or a common ground will lead your prospect to a certain conclusion: that you do not have the level of competence required to advise them. If you fail to provide adequate unique knowledge and offer your prospect value, then again, the outcome will be undesirable; while your prospect may really like you because you managed to build trust and understanding, if they sense that you are not competent, they may further perceive that you have some hidden motive and may become analytical of your intention.

If you want to be persuasive and easily gain the trust of people to the point that they are willing to take what you say at face value without over-analyzing every detail of every word you say, begin by becoming knowledgeable about your offer, find prospects and engage with them with friendly questions. Be sure to actively listen to them, be understanding and careful to build report and trust. Finally, make a reasonable request ('Will you join my business and let me help you become successful?"), and receive a reasonable response (How do I get started?).

My advice is to practice these skills in every area of your life, not merely in your business dealings. You can practice this technique all day long in various situations. Use the art of persuasion with every person you talk to by first finding common ground, build trust and be understanding by listening intently to them; offer advice or make recommendations and see if they take you upon it. As your confidence grows in this technique of persuasion don't be surprised if people begin asking for your advice all the time.

Have fun mastering the art of persuasion.

UNDETECTED MIND CONTROL

Are there mental control techniques?

Mental control techniques do exist and depending on their use, can become very flattering or counterproductive. Mental control has many meanings, so it can lend itself to certain confusions. It can be known as coercive persuasion, brainwashing, thought reform, manipulation, among others.

All these names share common elements, elements that define mental control. All refer to the persuasion and direct or indirect influence of the mind of an individual to fulfill a role. Next, we will define mental control promptly, specifying some of its techniques. Also, we will make clear who uses this type of mind control techniques and what their utilities are, both positive and negative.

Mind Control According To Steven Hassan

Under the umbrella of mind control include a series of techniques aimed at controlling and modifying the mental processes of an individual. These kinds of mind control techniques are no fantasy; in many cases, they are very effective and in certain cases irreversible. In spite of this, not all mental control is necessarily negative, since there are beneficial uses.

Mind control techniques can have very powerful effects. They can significantly influence an individual, in their actions, behaviors, thoughts, beliefs, tastes, relationships, and even in their own identity.

Researcher Steve Hassan makes a distinction between mind control and brainwashing. The distinction is in the consciousness of being manipulated or influenced. In brainwashing, the victim knows that he is being manipulated so that his thoughts change in favor of the aggressor. While, in mind control, the person need not be aware of the manipulation of the victim.

In this sense, mind control can be very subtle and sophisticated. Something that makes it dangerous, even when done with good intentions. Because someone, through mind control, can modify the way of being of other people without it being found out. The manipulator can be anyone, even someone very close.

Some mind control techniques

These mind control techniques are subtle and slow, that is, they do not have an immediate effect. Mental control is a long process that changes the mind of the manipulated gradually. Although this depends a lot on the techniques used, the duration of the application and the personal and social factors of the manipulation.

In addition, physical force is not necessary for the application of mind control techniques. However, there is a great psychological and social pressure on the manipulated. Anyone is susceptible to mind control. That is where the danger of misuse of these kinds of mental manipulations lies.

Some of the most well-known and effective mind control techniques are:

- **Total or partial isolation of the family or social nucleus.** Cutting with the affective ties of the possible manipulated facilitates the process of mental control since there is total or partial dependence on the manipulator.
- **Slow physical exhaustion.** Several activities are used to diminish the physical and cognitive abilities of manipulation. For example, forced labor or excessively long exercise days.
- **Change of diet.** An abrupt change in diet, especially decreasing protein also weakens the body and mind of the manipulated.

- **A constant reminder of simple or complex ideas.** This is one of the most important techniques, since only by keeping constantly in mind the ideas that want to be inserted in the manipulated, will the mental control be effective. This can be done orally, with songs and mantras, or in writing, with signs and mandatory readings.

- **Demonstrated measures of affection and rewards.** The manipulator gives attention and rewards to the manipulated as long as he does something that facilitates mental manipulation. All this to generate a dependency between the manipulated and the manipulator.

- **Subtle or direct use of drugs.** The use of narcotics is not mandatory, but it facilitates mental control.

- **Hypnosis.** To make the manipulated mind vulnerable, and in this way facilitate the manipulation process itself.

Who employ these techniques of mind control?

Mental control can be used by anyone who wants to manipulate or have influence over another individual. Also, those who use these techniques have very specific purposes, which can be political, social and/or personal. Because they seek an individual to lose their freedom of thought and personal particularities.

Therefore, mind control is generally employed by sects or cults. Using it to add new followers and keep members active. Being the leaders of the sects or cult who use the mental techniques with their followers.

Also, mind control techniques can be used by people with a low degree of empathy to manipulate and exploit another person. Although, you can also present some mental control between intimate relationships in which one of the parties abuses its power. As, for example, in relationships of: teacher / student, parents / children, boss / subordinate, doctor / patient, among others.

The usefulness of mind control techniques

Not all applications of these mind control techniques have a negative connotation. They can also be beneficial in certain circumstances, as long as they are not invasive or imposed.

When conscious doctors or psychologists employ these mind control techniques, they can be extremely beneficial in the lives of certain patients. It can be used to suppress an addiction, overcome a traumatic experience, improve self-esteem and even eliminate suicidal or self-destructive thoughts. In short, the techniques of mind control are not bad in themselves, they are only bad when they are used for evil purposes.

The Mental Control

Mind control does not indicate a special ability or control of the mind of others, the latter is manipulation.

Daily you face situations that can overwhelm you and provoke emotions that affect you negatively such as anger or envy. When you do not control the mind you can act or say things that are the result of anger, anger or any other emotion. Then you repent, of your words or acts, because that is not what you think.

Mental control is to become aware of your emotions and thoughts so that they are not protagonists in your behavior. It allows you to live situations calmly and helps you make decisions that help you The exercises to work mind control will help you to have a better perspective of your daily life.

Tips for working mind control

1. You are here and now in the present, connect with yourself and your environment. What happens is present, it has nothing to do with the past or future. React in the present.

2. Reflect, observe, do not get carried away by hypotheses or assumptions.

3. Work your empathy to be aware of the emotions of others as well as your own. That helps you develop your emotional intelligence.

4. Self-observation, do not act conditioned by emotions from another time. Do not get carried away by a badly evolved duel.

5. Live your life consciously. Eat and drink, walk and enjoy life, be aware of your breathing, work, feel, everything realizing what you do. Do not put your life on autopilot.

6. When you talk to others, do not think about what you are going to say. Listen and observe the words and attitude, which is sometimes more eloquent than what is said.

7. Practice meditation. To meditate is not to be relaxed and with a blank mind, it is also to observe thoughts and let them flow.

8. When you feel you are not in control, stop your reaction for a minute. Observe what is upsetting you.

The control of the mind and physical and emotional health interact with each other. If the mind is uncontrolled affects the emotional system, this, in turn, affects the physical state. In this way, a stressful mind, for your work or family life, can lead to digestive problems, muscle contractures and other conditions of your body. For these reasons, it is essential to have control of the mind to enjoy a healthy life.

Exercises to practice **mind control**

1. Breathe with a nasal inspiration counting to three, hold the other three breaths and expire at the same time. Practice this exercise five times to check your breathing.

2. Practicing mental games, such as successions of numbers or sudoku and logic games, is good training to speed up your brain system and redirect your mind, favoring concentration.

3. Change your hand to do some activity, this forces you to be attentive and focused when breaking the routine.

4. Learn something new to engage your brain.

5. Eat nuts, olive oil and add healthy fats like fish into your diet. Your brain needs these good fats.

It is important that you do not hurry, try to block the mind or fight against its thoughts, this is what hinders your work of mind control. Exercise some of these tips every day. When you control your mind, you will be the protagonist of your own life.

Do we control our thoughts or our thoughts control us?

The answer to this question is quite complex. In general terms, we would say that it depends on what you consider controlling. To clarify things, I'm going to divide my answer into three blocks:

1.   Impact of our thoughts on our emotions and behaviors

2.   How to control our thoughts so they do not control us

3.   The limits of our ability to control our mental content.

1.   Impact of our thoughts on our emotions and behaviors.

The Cognitive Hypothesis affirms that it is not situations, but thoughts, that determine our emotional response (this is not always the case, of course.) Other emotions are explained by other mechanisms, such as, for example, those derived from Classical Conditioning, or those caused by hormonal changes, or drugs, or alcohol, or fatigue and lack of sleep). But in many cases, there is an undoubted relationship between thought and emotion.

I will explain it with a joke once told by Salkovskis (a

renowned cognitive psychologist). Three men step on a poop. The first thinks: "This is a neighbor's dog and only wants to make my life bitter. I'm sure he has brought his puppy here to dirty my new shoes. He is always trying to annoy me." Obviously, the emotion this man will have will be anger. The second man steps on the poop and thinks: "I am unable to do anything right. I am an absolute disaster and I am going to make a mistake in all my life. I'm not worth anything. " The emotion, in this case, will be, in all likelihood, sadness. The third man thinks: "It's a good thing I did not put on my flip-flops!"; here the emotion that we all guess is joy, relief ...). The same thing happened to the three of them.

The effect of having an emotional response to a thought tends to make it more credible. It seems more real. It's like that because I feel it that way. In addition, once an emotional state is induced, the following thoughts are likely to be congruent with the emotional state, and one to distort things according to those emotions. For example, if the emotion is anger, I will begin to remember all the past grievances that person has caused me. And if it is sadness, I will repeat without ceasing all my list of failures and losses. So, I get into a loop in which thoughts and emotions reinforce each other to infinity. In this spiral, I can reach unimaginable heights.

The effect of the thoughts on us goes further.

Normally, from cognitive therapy, we understand that the combination of situation, thought and emotion is a trigger (in technical terms, a discriminative stimulus) for certain behaviors. Almost always, behaviors designed to reduce the emotional state if it is aversive, or to prolong it if it is pleasant. For example, the angry man will probably face the neighbor, to discharge his tension. The second, maybe go home, get in bed, and not go out all day. The third may celebrate it. Of course, these behaviors, being reinforced by a decrease in discomfort or by gratification, will tend to recur on future occasions.

The interesting thing is that the behaviors congruent with emotion tend to amplify it, and also to increase the credibility of the thoughts, and multiply them. For example, the man who gets into bed will probably end the day even more depressed and convinced of his low value. The enraged will fight with the neighbor that ends up convincing him that he is a bad person, etc ... We can get into a loop of thoughts, emotions, and behaviors that lead us to very unpleasant extremes, without knowing how it happened nor how to avoid it.

2. How to control our thoughts so they do not control us.

In Cognitive-Behavioral Therapy, we have a technique to detect and modify maladaptive thoughts that are controlling us in a negative way. This technique is Cognitive Restructuring.

To apply it, we begin by differentiating two types of thoughts:

Adaptive thoughts: they have two characteristics:

· **They help to confront a situation, even complex:** they give me courage, they serve me as positive self-instruction. 'I'm going to try it, come again, I'll get out of this one'.

· **They are realistic:** objective, descriptive (although they may include descriptions of unpleasant or negative things) Eg: this table is made of wood eg: I forgot the keys and I'm going to stay in the street

Disadaptive thoughts: they have two characteristics

  – They do not help to face a situation, because they generate anxiety or fear.
  – They are not realistic. They are not descriptive. That is, they contain valuations (judgments), interpretations or divination of the future (catastrophic anticipation) Eg1:

this table is horrifying (judgment). My boss has given it to me because he hates me (interpretation). This means that he plans to fire me (divination of the future). Eg2: I forgot the keys because I am a disaster that does not do anything right and I will end up alone and dead of cold under a bridge.

People tend to believe that both types of thoughts are realistic. They find it difficult to distinguish when they think badly. There are ways to help them distinguish when for is wrong, and change it for an adaptive one. This is what we call Cognitive Restructuring.

Cognitive Restructuring has 3 steps

·   **Logical Contrast -** I see if the thought contains judgments, interpretations or divination of the future. The interesting thing is that a maladaptive thought has traits that I can detect. These traits are what we call cognitive distortions. For example, it contains absolute terms (always, never, never, nothing, nobody), or labeling (idiot, bad person, useless) or talks about the future

·   **Empirical Contrast -** I look for evidence for and against my idea. A little below I give an example.

·   **Adaptive contrast -** I wonder if the thought helps me or is a terrorist who is boycotting me. This is necessary because sometimes we have thoughts that are logical, they are descriptive, they are empirically impeccable, but they do not help me at all. For example: "my daughter is going to die". It is absolutely realistic, it is not a badly formulated thought. But ... does it help me repeating it hour after hour every day? No, right? Well then, what I should do is detect it as maladaptive and discard it.

In cognitive restructuring, the idea is to identify harmful thoughts and change them for adaptive ones. For example, a child once told me: "I had a horrible day because I did everything wrong and everyone laughed all day about me". Empirical contrast: How many things have you done wrong today? How many children are there in your school and how many have laughed? How much time do you spend at school and how long have you laughed? Asking it turned out that he had failed to stop a goal and a couple of kids were teasing him a couple of minutes at recess. So the adaptive thinking would be: Today I missed a goal and so and so and I have been teased a couple of minutes at recess. It is not a pleasant situation, but neither is it so terrible.

The most inferential part of cognitive therapy is the one that tries to explain why some people have automatic adaptive thoughts in certain situations and others have maladaptive ones. The explanation is this: automatic thoughts are children of something that cognitive calls (mos) underlying beliefs or core ideas (learned) about themselves or the world. Many times, these beliefs are adaptive and adjusted; but, in some cases, people start from very harmful beliefs. For example, the second man in the joke may have a belief similar to this: "I am a worthless disaster, I will never succeed in anything that I propose, and I will fail in all my attempts. "

Belief works in the following way: whatever the situation, what you are going to think is congruent with the belief. And to maintain the credibility of the belief, you will tend to discard incongruous information and magnify the importance of the congruent. In other words: the cognitive distortions of maladaptive thoughts are errors in the processing of information so that the belief is maintained. For example, the first man in the joke seems to start from a belief that is Beware of people who are bad and will try to harm you. Before the event of stepping on a poop, what occurs to him is this is the neighbor's fault because this interpretation provides an explanation that is consistent with his belief. He does not realize that he has made a processing error, a cognitive distortion: in this case,

With cognitive restructuring, we get a person to detect their irrational thoughts, identify beliefs, and modify them to be adaptive.

However, I realized a couple of years ago with some patients who, sometimes, when they are already well restructuring, and already fully understand that their maladaptive thoughts are not real or logical and can reformulate them, these random thoughts continue to be very powerful.

What happens is that some maladaptive thoughts retain the emotional credibility (the ability to provoke an emotional response) when they no longer have rational credibility (we know they are absurd). Patients sometimes express it as they know that it is not true, but they feel it is real.

This happens because thoughts can also function as conditioned stimuli do. If we have thought something many times in an aversive context (fights, rejections, etc), it becomes a Conditional Stimulus (CS) capable of eliciting that emotional response. And, sometimes, as with other CDs, they re-sensitize (increase their ability to arouse discomfort) because patients tend to push them away when anxiety increases (hence the distraction would function as an escape behavior). By blocking them, they do not get used, they do not lose their emotional power.

When we have reached that point in which a thought no longer has rational credibility, It usually works as we work other Conditional Stimuli, that is, with the technique of the Exhibition. I make them repeat it millions of times (in all possible sensory levels: write it, record it and listen to it, say it, dance it) until it is boring, that is until it no longer produces that emotional response (in technical terms, we say that it gets used). Sometimes, I also contradict it: I make him say it with ridiculous voices (of Yoda, or of Topo Gigio) or sing it. What we intend with this is that, even if there is a maladaptive thought, it does not already have the capacity to awaken an emotional response.

3. The limits of our ability to control our mental content

As I suggested above, for a patient to be able to restructure maladaptive thoughts does not mean that they stop occurring. The brain is a machine to produce ideas without a filter. The brain works (for evolutionary reasons) providing explanations, interpretations, solutions, and answers in the form of brainstorming, but without discriminating whether they are adjusted or appropriate or not. In this sense, I can not control my mental content: I can not avoid that I can think of one thing or another. In fact, when we try to control our mental content, what we call camel effect occurs: thought increases in intensity and frequency. This is precisely the problem of Obsessive-Compulsive Disorder: patients try to not think certain things, and end up being unable to stop thinking about them.

However, if I am able to select what part of my mental

content I will give credibility and whatnot, if I have learned to reduce the emotional impact of certain thoughts, and to choose which ones I will allow them to direct my behavior or not , the one that occurs to me certain things stops being a problem. The thoughts are still there, but they no longer control me.

THE FOUR-PERSONALITY TYPES

How many types of personality human beings have is one of the most discussed topics in psychology. Understanding how others are is very useful to establish effective relationships with other people. How to identify each one has been researched for years by many experts and it seems that now a team has managed to divide it into several different classes.

Already in ancient Greece, Hippocrates postulated that every human being is composed of four senses of humor: a kind of basic substances whose mixture ended up giving rise to the personality of each. According to the Greek thinker, the proportion of blood, yellow bile, black bile, and phlegm could determine whether a person was braver, cranky, depressed or indifferent. An archaic theory that, however, for centuries served to explain how the human temperament worked until it was dismantled by scientific evidence.

But now the history of the study of human character seems to have taken an unexpected turn. A new study suggests that perhaps there are four types of personalities in which, in one way or another, we could see all reflected: average personality, reserved, egocentric and role model. These new data emerge from a study in which the profiles of more than 1.5 million people around the world have been analyzed through an alternative computational approach and data analysis techniques.

"The data obtained shows that there are higher densities of certain personality types ." explains William Revelle, professor of psychology at the Faculty of Arts and Sciences of Weinberg and lead author of this new research, published in the journal 'Nature Human Behavior'. A classification that, according to this new study, until now, "only existed in the literature of self-help and had no place in scientific journals ."

Although psychologists have long been quite skeptical of personality tests and their effectiveness, the large number of results recorded in this particular study indicates that experts could work with these new categories.

Average

This type was the most repeated in the questionnaires and we could call them normal. They show features of responsibility (conscience and consideration of a person) and kindness (understanding, little hostility) moderate, extroversion and emotional instability (or neuroticism: mood swings, tendency to feel angry or sad) a little more marked, and with low expectations (curiosity and search for new experiences and low learning).

Reserved

They are people with high levels of emotional stability linked to a normal character, neither open nor neurotic. They do not stand out for being extraverts, but they are kind and responsible. They are rather shy, do not usually look in the eyes and put great distances with others. Also, they are often quite insecure and keep information about their emotions (both positive and negative). Their disposition is usually empathic and correct.

Egocentric

According to scientists, these people are unpleasant for the rest. They combine a lower score in kindness, openness towards others and responsibility. They have a high degree of extraversion, but little frankness and scrupulosity. Also, they focus only on themselves and prefer not to live new experiences.

They think they know everything and impose their opinion on any subject. They show themselves superior, do not accept advice and always try to control the situation. According to the study, it is a toxic personality type, not only for others but for themselves as well. They only like the praises and refer to the great source of wisdom that they are at all times.

Role models

They have high levels of extraversion, kindness, and responsibility with a low degree of neuroticism. They are very open in every way, scrupulous. Traits that predominate in women and that would be cultivated with age. Also, they are always interested and take into account what others have to say. They are leaders and emotionally stable and hardworking.

The Northwestern researchers showed the classification to a skeptic of personality types, the professor of Psychology at the Faculty of Arts and Sciences of Weinberg William Revelle. "I will be very direct," he warned. "My first reaction was to say that this was nonsense ." However, he became interested to the point that he became the co-author of the study published in 'Nature'. "People have tried to classify personality types since the time of Hippocrates, but previous scientific literature has found that it makes no sense, now this data shows that there are higher densities of certain types, everything will change thanks to this study.", revealed to 'Time'.

Change over time

The researchers note that when the years pass there is an evolution. The data analyzed reveal something that everyone knows from their own experience: in adolescence, it is very common for us to be subjects centered on ourselves (especially men). However, over time, neurotic tendencies descend and increase responsibility and kindness.

The questionnaires used have between 33 and 400 questions and are reliable for a large number of people who have participated

When you study very large groups of people, clear trends appear that change according to the age group . The scientists defend that their conclusions will be of great help for psychologists and psychiatrists, that thanks to them they will have a reference model from which to diagnose mental illnesses.

What's cool is that a study with such a large data set would not have been possible before the internet, and before, maybe researchers would recruit students on campuses and maybe get a few hundred people. all these available online resources and more data can be shared.

In what type of personality do you fit?

Bad and good news. The bad news is that right now you could belong to any of the groups identified by this research, although you may not feel satisfied with the result. But the good news is that, according to the data thrown by this new study, the variable personality that can be modified over the years.

Some of the conclusions drawn from this study indicate that the characteristic features of self-centered people tend to be more densely concentrated among male adolescents, while those considered as role models increase as they grow. That is, the personality can improve over the years and the big data proves it.

NLP TECHNIqUES
TO MANIPULATE AND
PERSUADE PEOPLE

Neuro-Linguistic Programming (NLP) is a body of knowledge made up of two parts. The first is an attitude or philosophy, the second a set of tools and techniques created by that philosophy.

The simplest definition of the attitude is that 'subjective human experience has a structure that can be usefully manipulated.'

What does that mean? Well, 'subjective human experience' refers to each human's unique and personal experience of reality. For example, if three people are on board the same aircraft flying from London to New York, one might find the experience exciting, another very dull and the third terrifying. Even though each of them is doing roughly the same thing, they have their own unique and personal experience of it.

NLP takes the approach that this experience has a structure; it is not random but governed by rules and the law of cause and effect. If these rules are understood, then the experience can be usefully manipulated - turning fear into excitement for example.

Given this attitude, it is possible to experiment with the rules to see if a particular change in a person's experience will produce a particular effect. Once you discover that changing one thing systematically changes another, you have a technique that can be repeated. This is the second part of NLP - all the techniques and tools that have been created by experimentation with the structure of subjective experience.

An example of NLP

To experience NLP for yourself, try the following experiment. Read the instructions first, memorize the steps and then try them out.

1.   Close your eyes and think about someone that you love. Notice what image comes to mind when you think of this person. Pay attention to the feelings this image evokes and be aware of how intense they are.

2.   Pretend that you can push this image away into the distance until it looks small and far away. Be aware of any change in the intensity of your feelings about it.

3.   Pretend that you can bring the image close to you and make it larger and brighter. Again, be aware of

any change in the intensity of your feelings.

4.   Repeat steps 2 and 3 a few times and check whether they consistently produce the same result.

For many people who do this experiment pushing the picture further away decreases the intensity. Bringing it closer and making it larger is equally reliable in increasing the intensity of feeling. It does not matter if your experience is the same - each person's experience is different - but you should at least notice that changes in the way you see the image consistently and predictably affect how you feel about it.

So, your subjective experience - the image of the person you love - has a structure (it's size and distance from you) that can be usefully manipulated (varied to increase the intensity of pleasant feelings).

NLP Techniques

Since its beginnings in the 1970s, the attitude of NLP has been adopted by many people who have used it to conduct experiments. As a result, many techniques or patterns have been identified which predictably and usefully affect a person's subjective experience.

For example, the fast phobia cure is an NLP technique which predictably and usefully reduces the fear a person experiences when exposed to something that frightens them. This could be anything from a spider to an enclosed space to the experience of driving on a busy road.

There are many such techniques and they can be broadly classified into two groups.

Personal techniques allow a person to affect some part of their own experience. For example, NLP can be used by presenters and performers to put themselves in a confident and energetic state before going on stage. Other personal NLP techniques can help a person be more effective in setting goals, thinking clearly, motivating themselves and much more.

Communication techniques allow a person to affect how they interact with others. NLP includes techniques for building rapport and trust with other people, for persuading them and for hypnotizing them.

A brief history of NLP

NLP was first developed in the 1970s by two men. John Grinder was a linguistics professor and Richard Bandler a computer scientist. Much of the development came from studies the two men made of successful people. They identified various patterns and structures that were present in the way these people behaved, thought and experienced the world. That process of studying or modeling formed much of the attitude of NLP and the resulting patterns formed many of the techniques.

Among the first group of successful people studied were several outstanding therapists. These included Fritz Perls, the Gestalt therapist, Virginia Satir, the family therapist and psychiatrist and hypnotist Dr.Milton Erickson. As such, many of the early NLP patterns had a significant therapeutic element and many of the early adopters of NLP were therapists.

Over time however the technology has advanced and is now increasingly popular with all kinds of people include salespeople, managers, trainers and those interested in self-development.

In Summary

NLP is both an attitude and a collection of techniques created by that attitude. It centers on that belief that subjective human experience has a structure that can be usefully manipulated. Experiments based on this belief have created many techniques. These allow a person to influence and affect themselves and others more effectively. From early beginnings in the 1970s, NLP has grown to be accepted and practiced worldwide.

NLP technique: mirroring and synchronization

There is usually a fundamental prerequisite for any successful communication: synchronization. The term comes from NLP. What does it mean exactly? So that your interlocutor can listen and interpret what you say you must somehow be in the same world as him, at the same level, on the same wavelength.

But how to make one feel that one is in the same state of mind as him (especially if it is not the case)? For example, it is difficult to hold a conversation for more than 2 minutes when one of the people is seated, totally relaxed, and the other is standing, firm, dominant: there is desynchronization.

Faced with this kind of situation, where the interlocutors are out of sync, NLP offers a formidable technique: mirroring. It is not too much to say that it is a prerequisite of synchronization, which is to adopt a position similar to that of your interlocutor and to evolve at the same pace as him. Warning! The goal is not to sync or to caricature his interlocutor! But above all to put in the same dynamics as him.

One must be careful when using the techniques of Neuro-Linguistic Programming, and not take everything literally. The term mirroring refers to a mirror, but you should not reproduce all the gestures, movements or expressions of the other as if you were his reflection. First, simply be careful not to take a position opposite to his: if he sits, do not stand ... If he leans forward to talk to you, do not stay back supported on your chair ... In short, do not try at all costs to assert your singularity by taking poses that are too original or out of sync with the mood that emerges from his behavior, draw on his attitude.

How to put this advice into practice, which may seem rather technical? First of all, do not worry: it's not so technical, you just have to try it the first time, then practice! You will improve quickly.

Here is a little fun exercise to do on the bus or subway: synchronize with the person sitting in front of you: cross your arms, play with your mobile ... exactly as it does ... Then, to test the quality of this synchronization, touch your nose as if you were itching ... If the person also has the hand to his face, it is won! According to NLP, this means that you have established the first level of synchronization. Congratulations!

Manipulation by NLP technique? How to see through negotiation tricks!

NLP is controversial. Skeptics criticize that NLP as a psycho-method purely aims to manipulate people. Others see NLP as a mix of techniques that can help you make quick money. The fact is: NLP techniques are becoming increasingly important in the business world. It can not hurt to know how NLP works to protect itself against manipulation and nasty tricks. In this post, we'll tell you what's behind NLP, which are the best-known techniques, and how to spot and fend them off.

With the right negotiation techniques to success

Negotiations are part of everyday life in project management. Your clients, supervisors and team members have conflicting interests, so conflicts are inevitable. As a project leader, you have to make sure that negotiations are solution-oriented and that, in the end, a win-win situation is created for all participants - but without being manipulated.

The right negotiation techniques will help you! The EVEREST method, for example, helps you prepare for the trial, strong rhetoric and safe body language give you sovereignty - as we have reported in other posts. However, to be able to see through your opponent and deliberately ward off manipulation, it is helpful to know and be able to react to the NLP technique.

NLP - what is that?

NLP stands for Neuro-Linguistic Programming and originated in the 1970s in a research project at the University of Santa Cruz in California. The Americans Richard Bandler and John Grinder found in the observation of communication professionals similarities. They then developed techniques to change people's behavior and communication.

One of the most important NLP developers, Robert Dilts, describes NLP as a behavioral model that examines the patterns that arise through the interaction of brain, language, and body. Our language influences our perception and thus our emotional and mental experience. A conscious use of language, therefore, makes it possible to read these patterns of behavior and to harmonize one's behavior with the patterns of other people.

NLP, therefore, aims to better understand its interlocutor and to make positive changes to it - manipulating it a bit to avoid communication hurdles, conflicts or the like. That's why the concept of neuro-linguistic programming:

- Neuro: brain - perception through the sensory organs and processing in the brain
- Linguistic: language and body - verbal and nonverbal communication
- Programming: change of known thought and behavior patterns

Assumptions of neuro-linguistic programming

NLP is based on certain assumptions, that is, ways of

thinking that are accepted as important by NLP users. Some assumptions of the NLP are for example:

People react to their subjective perception, not to external reality.

People make the best choice based on the information available.

Human behavior is based on a positive intention.

People can learn to do something specific when other people can.

People have all the resources to achieve the desired change.

How to recognize and ward off NLP techniques in everyday business

There are a lot of NLP techniques. Today, we'll introduce you to five of the best-known, so that you are prepared for when your negotiator tries to manipulate you with one of these techniques.

1. Analog marking

This technique describes the targeted use of verbal and non-verbal language, for example, by emphasizing keywords or building tension moments. Three ways in which your counterpart uses this technique are, for example:

- Use of pauses to make what is said work

- Variation Speech rate to ward off your boredom

- Change in the pitch by going up or down at the end of the sentence to create a command or question character

2. Anchor

The Anchor Technique aims to ensure that we humans always respond to any stimulus that is perceived by one of our five senses of seeing, hearing, smelling, tasting, or feeling with the same behavior and are therefore influenced by it. Three examples from everyday working life would be:

- Somebody is knocking on your shoulder - that gives you appreciation.

- You are shown a holiday picture - that awakens your joy.

- Someone describes a bridge to you, although you are afraid of heights - that causes fear in you.

3. Pacing

Under pacing, NLP users understand to go in the same step as his interlocutor. This means that your counterpart tries to mirror your behavior in order to build trust and a positive atmosphere of conversation. Your conversation partner achieves this, for example by:

• Imitation of your own body language - without being affected

• Taking your own voice

• Adaptation to your breathing rhythm

4. Leading

Leading means leading your conversation partner. So if your interlocutor has trusted you by pacing him, he will begin to change trifles in his behavior. If you accept the behavior now and join in the way he wants, he has you in your pocket - you are being manipulated! So pay attention to the changes in the behavior of your conversation partner during the conversation.

5. Disney strategy

This method goes back to the world-famous Walt Disney, who was a man of strong dreams, always subdividing his goals into three phases. Similarly, the Disney strategy works by looking at a situation from three different angles to increase creativity in conversation and to gain new insights. Watch if your negotiating partner suddenly takes on one of the three roles of a dreamer, realist or critic:

• The dreamer is subjectively oriented but does not make a practical judgment about an idea.

• The realist is more pragmatic and develops plans for further action.

• The critic scrutinizes guidelines and practices criticism to identify errors.

NLP In Brief

Think positive

Neurolinguistic Programming (NLP) examines the relationships between body, language, and thought programs. NLP coaches claim that this will make it possible to significantly increase performance in leadership and communication. It is attached to the psyche and tries to change obstructive thinking programs positively (reframing). Example: Perfectionists should learn to accept a mistake. Including all sensory channels and the body, negative emotions should be transformed into positive ones. According to NLP, the positive attitude towards a colleague or interlocutor is the basis for good communication. In the NLP many elements of behavioral therapy and hypnosis are used.

Originated in the USA

NLP was launched in the US in the 1970s by Gestalt psychologist Richard Bandler and linguist and linguist John Grinder. They wanted to know how top-level communicators deal with other people, how they manage to convince others. They analyzed the three distinguished American therapists Fritz Perls, Virginia Satir, and Milton Erickson. The individual elements of their success, such as their behavior and movements, were summarized by Bandler and Grinder in the NLP. They also developed an NLP-specific language. About five years ago, the NLP scene established itself in Germany.

Anchoring, Pacing, and Leading

Anchoring means linking a feeling with a picture, sound or touch. The stimulus and the reaction, similar to the classical conditioning, are coupled with each other. That is, a certain feeling comes up automatically when, for example, a certain part of the body is touched. During pacing, the same posture is taken during a conversation as the other person is doing to build a good wire. To convince the other, the posture is slightly changed (Leading/lead). According to the NLP, this is the basis for a successful negotiation. Sellers like to use this technology.

Not everyone can become an NLP Expert

Technician or Practitioner?

Since NLP is easy to learn, anyone can become an NLP technician. An NLP technician is someone who has little or no interest in being of service to others or helping people excel, but is more interested in using NLP to manipulate people or to generate business with it. These could be people who have just read about NLP or have done some formal NLP training, or they may even be certified NLP Trainers themselves. Believe it or not, there are NLP Trainers who care more about their back pocket than they do about their students. They teach or use NLP incongruently, or primarily as a way to generate income.

Don't worry, NLP technicians are easy to identify, here's what to look out for:

- They don't walk their talk...
- They may use NLP to manipulate, influence and persuade others against their will.
- They are easily stressed, unsettled or ungrounded.
- They have personal and/or professional relationship problems.
- They habitually indulge in food and/or substances that are damaging to their health.

- They may often be unwell due to burnout or negligence of their health.
- They are not good listeners.
- They try to be smart, boast or one-up in their communication.
- They try to convince you to buy their product or service.
- They are self-interested and generally ego-driven.
- They don't demonstrate alignment with the NLP Presuppositions.

The kind of person described above is someone who says one thing and does another. They may even be good at some NLP skills, but they don't earn your trust. NLP technicians are not aware of their deeper potential and/or appreciative of what connects us as human beings. This awareness is, however, clear to anyone who has mastered the NLP skills and lives in alignment with the NLP Presuppositions.

Genuine NLP Practitioners and Trainers can be identified as people who:

- Walk their talk...
- They respect each individual's values
- They have other people's best interests at heart when using NLP
- They are calm, approachable, warm and friendly

- They are stable, balanced and emotionally intelligent
- They are at cause in their relationships (as opposed to being at effect)
- They are in control of their behaviors
- They are mostly well and energetic
- They are good listeners
- They treat everyone equally
- They encourage you to find your own best answers
- They naturally inspire people
- They have a genuine interest in adding value to the experience of others
- They apply the NLP Presuppositions when doing NLP and aim to live in alignment with them.
- NLP technicians pull strings, ethical NLP'ers build relationships based on trust. NLP technicians do the things that NLP skills and presuppositions are designed to help people overcome.
- NLP is a powerful psychological tool, but like most tools, it can be constructive in the hands of some and destructive in the hands of others.
- Genuine NLP Practitioners are people who are certified by genuine NLP training providers. They have not only read books on the subject or have done online training. They appreciate

that NLP is about people and they are inclined to reach out and make a difference. Those who have mastered NLP use their skills ethically and congruently, no matter where or with whom they are using their skills.

Perhaps being able to model excellence and replicate it (which is central to NLP), doesn't mean being able to live it all the time and everywhere yourself. Even the founders of NLP are not flawless, and so aren't many well-meaning NLP Practitioners and Trainers, but that doesn't mean they're technicians and it's not a reason not to be even more curious about the brilliance of NLP.

In summary:

NLP is easy to learn, but those who learn it, for this reason, are likely to be NLP technicians. Those who learn it because they want to enjoy greater control and freedom over their state of mind, responses and interactions with others are likely to be authentic and trustworthy NLP'ers.

PERSUASION

Persuade or convince? The hidden meaning

In this book, we talk about the weapons of persuasion those techniques between NLP and Kung Fu thanks to which you can sell more, at a higher price and incidentally conquer a girl.

You will surely have happened to attend a seminar, read a book or even watch a video on YouTube about these wonderful characters that focus teaching on negotiation techniques on neuro-linguistic programming as if Richard Bandler and John Grinder had invented it to sell door-to-door vacuum cleaners.

No, NLP serves to recondition certain sides of the character with the aim of solving people's psychological problems. Any different use is an exercise in rhetorical art in which attempts are made to favor certain reactions to stereotyped behavior. If you can do it, if you know how to do it, you can take your caller where you want and basically close a deal to your advantage or just win a girl. If we talk about these practices we enter the domain of persuasion that we will now try to define.

What Is Persuasion?

Persuading someone to do something means letting them make a decision based on an emotional push and in any case not filtered by the rational mind according to the logic of calculating the advantage/disadvantage ratio. Since we cannot have the rational control of all the instances that characterize a considered choice, according to some all the purchasing decisions take place with a substantial lack of knowledge, therefore finding ourselves to reel in a sea of unknowns, it would be the emotional part to have the last word, not the rational, ignorant by nature of things.

Once the people marketing have realized this fundamental truth that is we do not know why Audi is better than Alfa Romeo, they have begun to study ways to reinforce this ignorant prejudice, not letting us see the characteristics of the engine or telling us about the road holding, but through a creeping communication that over the years has created a distance between Italian and northern European cars that are certainly better, right? Do you know why? All the fault of the brand positioning, the good ones would say ... and there is.

What does it mean to convince?

The conviction is instead a much more complex procedure, which at times I doubt belongs to the human race, perhaps more tied to teaching than to rhetoric. Convincing means making a journey that leads you to conclude (win) together with your interlocutor. In practice, you make a reasoned path that leads you and the other to come with that 3 + 3 is 6 as long as we count in base 10, otherwise, it makes 10 in base 6 ... more or less.

You have already understood that marketers cannot convince anyone because of a lack of resources, in fact, no medium can be so hot as to allow a massive and at the same time effective educational function. There is no other way than the shortcut of persuasion, which bypasses any rational defense by intercepting primitive, acquired and now easy to recognize drives. It works, of course, it works, but it's not like you can take the poo of a guinea pig, put it in a jar and sell it as caviar, at least not forever.

How much time do you need?

Think of a long-term perspective in which you allow your target audience and yourself to speak clearly, to establish a relationship based on things, not on what is said or what we think of things, but on things, those what people need and what you do for people. There are no creeping ideas to pass through colorful spots shot on the island that is not there, the communicators must not be hucksters , but interlocutors, bringing forward a healthy attitude towards confrontation on concrete issues, on problems to be solved, not on how to survive in a difficult world or how to tie the knot to get the blood flowing to the brain.

The persuaders recognize them easily because when you ask them something, they do not respond.

Why do we end up saying 'YES': persuasion or manipulation?

Many think that persuasion and manipulation are the same.

It must be said that all of us are constantly bombarded by door-to-door salesmen, unscrupulous and ill-intentioned, who implement strategies of every kind to make us capitulate in a purchase, without even being aware of what is happening to us, and to end up to bring home a product, only to realize that we didn't need it at all.

Like all of us in life, we have been persuaders and manipulators. Each of us used our communication, to convince others with our ideas and convictions, both for the approval of a project in the workplace and for the choice of the restaurant to go to and to choose the film to watch the Saturday night and much more.

We have all tried to convince someone to do something that was only pleasing to us.

As a real estate consultant, I asked myself how to persuade people without manipulating them. Both because I firmly believe in the responsibility I have in this job and because manipulation does not lead to any result.

When someone manages to sign a contract against

their will, we are faced with manipulation. Being a manipulator means getting burned: news circulates fast and your reputation is seriously compromised in a short time.

My desire instead was only to have effective communication tools, with the intention of being able to carry on a negotiation where both parties came out satisfied. This means that over time you create a good reputation; this, in turn, is a powerful generator of relationships and empathy: we trust a person referenced and of whom everyone speaks well.

And so psychology gave me a hand.

Is persuading and manipulating the same thing? The answer is no, that's why.

Persuasion is trying to convince someone of something, taking into account both the needs and needs of our client in order to achieve common goals.

A relationship is therefore established "I win, you win", that is my intention includes both a benefit for you and the achievement of my goal, this benefit can be defined as equivalent. There is, therefore, a positive intention that wants a true and significant improvement in the life of both. In this way we recommend, we suggest something to someone.

Instead, manipulating is trying to impose something on someone, taking into account only their own needs and their gain or profit, in an "I win, you lose" relationship.

In this case, there is an induction to do something, also using incorrect means (omission of data and/or documents). A very strong term.

As you can see two meanings therefore with a very different weight if you think that in the first there is a simple suggestion, while in the second a much stronger word is used, induction.

What differentiates persuasion and manipulation is the intention behind the action of conviction.

There are various linguistic tools and communication techniques (such as reading body language) to be more convincing. But, as I have already said, the techniques are only mere tools and it is the one who uses them that determines intentions, results, and effectiveness. Likewise, the same language tools can be persuasive or manipulative.

As can be inferred, it is the intention that underlies the action that makes the difference. The instrument can also be the same.

The amoral seller who uses a certain linguistic tool to trim an apartment with manufacturing defects tries to manipulate the client and the reality of the facts. But the same linguistic tool can be used to make a good investment or solve a problem for our client.

The difficulty in distinguishing between the two meanings lies in the fact that two people can apparently behave in the same way, but it is their intention that completely changes the meaning of their gesture.

It is therefore clear that learning persuasive techniques to be used in everyday life is important: because it makes it easier for us to help others, in the event that we find ourselves facing people who are unable to make a decision deemed right.

Experts like Paul Ekman in reading body language, such as Robert Cialdini in the field of psychology of persuasion, have provided us with many useful tools, both to defend ourselves from certain situations and to be used to be more convincing or to make a benefit to others.

In conclusion: what distinguishes persuasion from manipulation is the intention. Those who try to persuade want a sincere common benefit. Anyone who wants to manipulate only aspires to personal gain.

Psychology of engagement: persuading and convincing

Being able to communicate effectively depends a lot on the content and the target audience. Effectiveness is measured through the actions that people make in the face of specific communication and the suggestions that accompany it. In addition to the quality of communication, there are other factors that strongly affect the desired actions.

We live influenced. It is clear that the world of advertising and consequently that of sales has a high psychological component and uses strategies to achieve a concrete behavior in the recipient of the message or to change attitudes that in turn will succeed in modifying other future behaviors. The first case refers for example to the sale of a certain product, such as a car. In the second one, it refers to, for example, traffic campaigns to avoid alcohol consumption while driving.

But not only are these strategies used for commercial purposes, as we advanced in this book on telemarketing but also on a day-to-day basis we use them within our common social behavior to achieve our objectives, sometimes consciously and others unconsciously. We all use social influence or persuasion constantly. For example, when we want to pass some notes of a subject, when we try to convince someone to approach us by car somewhere, or go to a certain bar that night, etc.

When we speak of persuasion we cannot fail to mention the greatest expert in this field: Robert Cialdini. His book masterpiece " The weapons of persuasion " (1984) has been cited in tens of thousands of articles and books in recent decades. It represents the clearest and most convincing work on the levers that are adopted to seduce and persuade people to take action.

The six heuristics listed in his best-seller work and are often used online, by individuals, organizations or e-commerce. We cannot define cheating or scams these techniques, as all the information we pass through communication channels, even if they are often used for that purpose. If used ethically and honestly, they should be understood and used to strengthen our communication. Because these levers are to be disapproved only if the information given is false or groundless. For those who do not know them yet, these six techniques can also be used for a good purpose, if they contain truthful and correct information. I illustrate them by adapting them to the world of digital communication.

The six heuristics of online persuasion

1) Commitment and consistency: Consistency is appreciated by the people who look at us. Psychologists have long understood the importance of the "principle of coherence" in directing human actions. Prominent theorists, such as Leon Festinger, Fritz Hieder, and Theodore Newcomb, consider the need for consistency a central factor in motivating behavior. Being consistent is not for everyone, we must have a strategic direction in mind and keep it for the time necessary to make it clear to those who see us that we are committed to communicating a certain position well. Consistency is a double-edged sword, it could also be used against us and our positions. Personal communication always starts from a strategic positioning decision (the same thing also happens for products) and sudden change, without clearly communicating it, makes us appear weak and unreliable.

2) Reciprocity: Generally the man feels the need to reciprocate real favors, or presumed such. A small initial favor may lead to reciprocate with a significantly larger favor. One of the many applications of this lever is the refolding-after-refusal . Imagine that you want me to agree to grant an interview; they ask me in many and often I refuse for lack of time. One way to facilitate the operation would be to make me a greater request first, for example, the free participation in an event, which in all likelihood I will refuse and, after my refusal, present the minor request that you had in mind from the beginning: "then give me a small interview, just three questions " .

We can observe a small example of reciprocity on asynchronous social media, like Twitter or Instagram, where following certain people produces the effect of replacing the follow.

3) Social proof: People, on average, tend to consider behaviors or choices made by a large number of people more valid. Robert states that there is "an important clarification on the principle of social proof: we use the actions of others to decide what is the right behavior also on our part, especially when these others appear similar to us" . If everyone follows a certain character, it means that it could also be useful to me if everyone buys a certain smartphone, it means that it is solid, performing and fashionable. If the restaurant is full you eat well. We can verify the principle of social proof in any field, from YouTube videos to blog post sharing. The signal that a given person is important or says authoritative things is often placed in the amount we see below.

There is an interesting snowball effect that you can see on your most popular updates. For example, the more people like and share your Facebook update, the greater the likelihood that other users will go, with the benefit of the algorithm which is also based on this variable.

The brain is just a "lazy piece of meat," says US neuroscientist Gregory Berns. Often and more willingly we entrust our decisions to others to save time and intellectual energy and the "social proof" feeds on this predisposition.

4) Authority: The assertions supported by a reference to a prominent figure, real or presumed, increase their persuasive value. Fame increases authority in one field, the position held makes one person more authoritative than another. Whoever manages to be perceived as an opinion leader on a given topic has a clear road to the credibility front. It is not easy to apply this lever immediately, because it takes years to affirm it. A practical thing you can do right away is to take advantage of the authority reflected by other industry leaders. For example, a blogger who mentions a character recognized as a Guru in his field, will be considered reliable and taken into greater consideration by virtue of the confirmation of the authority of the subject.

5) Sympathy: That is the construction of a bond of sympathy and similarity, real or presumed, between persuader and persuaded. Being accessible, well-disposed and relaxed in behavior and relationships brings people together. I trust those who welcome me and transmit tranquility to me and create the conditions for a harmonious relationship.

We care about gravitating around people who reflect our opinions, values, interests or what we believe in and who we believe to be important and positive. It is very important to create your own audience, personalized on your Brand identity and engage in the narration of your own values (those interested should read: " How to select your social media follow-up"). This gives you confidence in your content and increases engagement and interaction with them.

6) Scarcity: This leverage relies on the natural tendency to optimize the availability of resources of a given asset, induces to the purchase if the availability of the asset is presented as limited in time or in its accessibility.

If you attend larger e-commerce sites, you will see this heuristic in action. Messages like "only two remain", "the offer expires in 5 hours" or "other 5 people are viewing this hotel room" are the most concrete examples that will instinctively lead you to think that if you arrive later you can't get the place, the discount or the product.

People are more likely to take action, participate or buy if they are convinced that time and quantity are limited. The perception of scarcity automatically creates a sense of urgency that cancels the cold analytical reasoning.

This summary of the levers that I move the action is only a part of those exposed by Robert Cialdini. There are others that I have not mentioned as the contrast principle, or to show what one wants to sell only after a series of poor preparatory products. For a further deepening of the theme, I suggest you read this important text on persuasion well. Taking care to use these techniques only correctly and honestly with others. Because true persuasion comes from the reliability of thought and action. Those who behave incorrectly, even if at first can get good results, cannot stand the test of time.

The 5 Secrets Of Persuasive Communication

Persuasion was defined by the great philosopher Aristotle as the art of inducing people to do things they would not normally do if we did not ask them.

As I mentioned earlier, the ability to persuade is of considerable importance in everyday life, both in the personal and professional world, often determining the success of our initiatives.

Who among us does not know at least one person with a great persuasive spirit? The persuasive subjects are those able to win the consent of others in any circumstance, gaining total approval and convincing them to act in a certain way.

A question arises spontaneously: are persuasive ones born or do they become? Both options are correct. This gift can be innate or learned through specific training courses.

Almost every day we feel the need to convince those around us to accept our point of view without hesitation or to accept our request kindly. We have started to engage in this activity since we were children, refining the most effective techniques by hand, and we still try to direct the judgment of others in our favor, although aware of the growing difficulties.

The long experience in the business world has made me understand that the capacity for persuasion can bring enormous benefits in terms of communication: it is a sort of magic formula that helps us manage interpersonal relationships, positively influencing opinions, attitudes, and actions of others.

Below you will find 5 secrets that will allow you to attract, fascinate and convince your interlocutors in a really effective way. Let's see them together!

1. Use The Explosive Mix Empathy + Sincerity

Empathy + Assertivity = Persuasion.

The famous Aristotelian pathos theorized over 2000 years ago, and modernly known as empathy, today represents a crucial factor in social relations. Being empathetic means putting ourselves on the same level as the interlocutor to understand the way in which he sees and lives a certain situation, or more generally, the world around him.

To exercise empathy it is necessary to listen with the heart as well as the mind, to learn to read the emotions of others, to put oneself in their shoes. Some people are naturally inclined to feel empathy and therefore able to use it effectively; they predict how others will behave in a certain circumstance by placing themselves on their wavelength, and consequently, they know how to express themselves.

When there is empathy, a spontaneous feeling of trust will inevitably take place. The ability to transmit trust is a factor that should not be underestimated due to its great importance on a psychological level. Whoever proves to be truly sincere, giving proof of having the problems of others at heart, gives a different tone to the conversation, stimulates the receptivity of the interlocutor and induces him to open up. This is why the mix of empathy and sincerity will help you develop your persuasive communication to the fullest.

2. Actively Listen To People

The good listener is a kind of magnet that magically draws others to himself.

Generally, we prefer to speak rather than listen, convinced that people who are predisposed to listening are those who have nothing interesting to say. Wrong observation! Think of a friend who does not pay attention to what you say. It's really frustrating, isn't it?

Active listening is one of the most important aspects of communication: effective persuasion arises precisely from the ability to listen, which does not mean to remain silent while the others speak. Active listening generates good private and working relationships, improving them over time, helping us to understand the thoughts and emotions of our interlocutors, and maintaining high mutual attention.

Active listening is a very complex task that requires concentration and training, but at the same time, it is a necessary condition for learning. Active listening is also a confirmation gesture that increases the self-esteem of the speaker; the lack of listening, instead, generates the opposite effect.

What can you do to show your partner that you are really listening to him? Here are some tips:

A.   Don't interrupt it;

B.   Don't complete his sentences;

C.   Don't offer too hasty advice;

D.   Intervene in the most opportune moment.

*

3. Keep High Attention To Your Interlocutor

Lack Of Attention = Ineffective Communication = Zero Results

Attention can only be obtained when there is interest.

If you want your message to be heard, you must arouse enough interest in people to keep the attention alive. Getting a constant level of interest is very difficult for one simple reason: several studies have proven that the time frame in which we can stay focused on a certain topic is quite limited.

How can you move to encourage others to listen to you? What can you do to keep your contact person's attention? You have to make sure that they are interested in what you are saying, to prevent boredom from taking over.

If you have to make a request or give a speech it is essential that you get your message understood on the first try. The preliminary phase lays the foundations for the good or the bad outcome of the communication.

When you realize that the attention of your interlocutor has dropped, try to find out why. Is your speech boring? Did you miss something important? Have you used a language that is too sectorial and therefore incomprehensible?

Here are some valid moves that I tested first in the field:

A.   The speech begins with a particular anecdote;

B.   Ask provocative questions;

C.   Propose a brainstorming session;

D.   Tell about your personal experiences;

E.   Give concrete examples;

F.   Help yourself by showing pictures.

4. Beware Of Your Body Language

Make your body express the right message.

Why is non-verbal communication so important? Interactions between human beings do not occur exclusively through speech and listening. Even when we talk and listen we express feelings and emotions through body language, assuming postures and making gestures that convey a strong meaning. It is important to learn to read these signals to communicate persuasively and to give the right force to your speech.

Non-verbal behavior determines the impression we have of others and what they have of us. All industry experts agree that the interpretation of human attitudes is based primarily on visual factors, followed by vocal factors and only the contents of the messages last.

If the interlocutor finds consistency between your facial expressions and the words you speak he will be led to feel a greater feeling of trust towards you, letting yourself be influenced more easily. If instead, your expressions contradict your words, it will tend to close and get away from you.

What are the negative signs of body language to avoid?

A.   Don't fold your arms or cross your legs when you're sitting, because it will seem like you want to stay on the defensive.

B.   Smile at the people you talk to because a positive gesture will help you achieve equally positive results.

C.   Keep direct eye contact with your interlocutor, because you will show interest and attention.

5. Exploit The Power Of Words

Success can depend on the right words spoken at the right time.

Do you know the power that words play in everyday interactions? Are you aware that some are effective and others less effective? Putting together the right words is a subtle art that is often ignored or otherwise overlooked.

The construction of discourse and the terms used have a direct effect on the outcome of the communication process and determine its success or failure. The psycholinguistics precisely studies the effects that words produce on the mind and human emotions.

Imagine you want to communicate something to your hypothetical interlocutor: you have in mind an image that you have to translate into words. As a sender, you send the message to the receiver, who then translates the words back into an image, to which he attributes a personal meaning that may not be the same as yours.

If the mental image your interlocutor has constructed is different from yours, the communication process will be ineffective. This feedback will, therefore, help you understand how to take action to improve the content of the message.

My advice is to adopt an open communicative style: it favors confrontation, as it does not set rigid rules and allows you to be more flexible. Open communication will encourage others to adopt your own point of view.

Conclusion

Persuasive communication is the main ingredient of personal and professional success, an expressive modality that combines Assertiveness and Empathy.

Knowing how to communicate persuasively means winning the attention, interest, and trust of the people you have in front of you.

6 TECHNIQUES OF MIND MANIPULATION YOU CAN LEARN

Manipulate people: Everyone does it & that's how it works for you!

If you want to learn to manipulate, you have to be prepared in principle to make others into externally determined marionettes in the game for your own goals? If you do not want to be manipulated, you should learn the technique of your enemies.

Manipulation is a learnable technique with a conceivably negative image. Manipulating evil people to achieve their goals, good people communicate. If that were indeed the case, we would have to resign ourselves to living in a world full of evil people and being bad people ourselves.

1. Is manipulating evil?

All manipulate - consciously or unconsciously - and everyone should deal with it, at least to protect themselves from involuntary influence on their own behavior. But mastery of manipulative techniques can also help you reach your own goals and make your life more enjoyable without automatically misleading or mistreating others. Within the categorical imperative, one can develop a moral guideline for one's own (manipulative) behavior that prevents you from becoming a man-despising arsehole.

Is it so reprehensible to take some measures so that the new colleagues in the workplace find you sympathetic? Or skilfully deal with the parents more pocket money by clever action? To suggest to the teacher that you are a good student? To raise a salary increase for the boss? To increase an increased willingness to help nurses in the hospital? Media, advertising, politics, church - they all work consciously with manipulative techniques and your friends, loved ones and other people often do this unconsciously. You can only handle it confidently if you know the tricks and you can recognize them as such.

2. The first impression: Manipulate how others see you!

A situation that we all have to constantly encounter again and again is the famous first impression we make. Of course, you often get a second and even a third chance in life, but who can handle the psychological effects of the first impression virtuoso, facilitates life in many ways - regardless of whether it is the first date, the job interview or the hiring an apartment is. It has been proven that the first impression of a human being decisively determines how the human brain arranges and interprets all subsequent experiences and impressions with this person. You can use that 'morally harmless' to the benefit. You have between 0.3 and 7 seconds to charm the other person and you do less with what you say.

• Attitude and gait! With a stable, upright posture you will not only impress the other person, but the posture will also affect you and you will feel more confident. You can practically practice this by consciously assuming first your normal posture, then a decidedly sloppy-limp and then an extremely upright posture. Run around in space in these attitudes, drawing comparisons, examining in the mirror and watching your sensations. Concentrate exactly on the positions of your head, your hands, arms, and shoulders.

• Handshake! The screw clamp is uncomfortable, flabby and sweaty too. Consider which handshake was well received by you and tries to imitate its quality.

• Eyes! Look your opponent in the face, thinking of something you like. The eyes are the window to the soul.

• Position of the feet! Feet aimed at the counterpart are read as interest. Show your feet to the side and only the body is frontal, the negative is perceived. However, it is said that for a new get-to-know, it is best to take a slightly oblique-lateral attitude and the counterpart not to move frontal and close to the people. Leave enough space and allow the other person to move closer if they wish.

3. The halo effect - create a halo

The halo effect is a measurable cognitive distortion in which human cognition draws conclusions about known characteristics of persons for unknown properties. It could be observed that these mechanisms work similarly when we meet new people. The first character traits that we experience overshadow and dominate the way we classify and perceive all other personal information. For this reason, it is highly manipulative when you tell others in advance of a still unknown person - it affects significantly how this person is then perceived. Many brands take advantage of this effect by overemphasizing a few positive features of their products, so that other, poorer properties are less perceived.

• Think about which of your characteristics is the most meaningful in each context.

• Seek ways to emphasize this quality to you.

4. Practice reading people in the art

If you want to successfully manipulate someone, you need to understand how he or she is ticking. You must learn to observe others and understand the signs. Empathy is a means of trying that because if you can empathize with others, you also understand their strengths and weaknesses better. Not everyone is equally equipped with this ability, then it is useful to observe closely and to distinguish at least basic types of people:

- ***The rational types:*** they are open to argumentation, to logical thinking, like to control their emotions. When you want to manipulate these people into a certain behavior, it is rarely useful to address their emotions. In these cases, you must take a rational approach and, above all, make the person feel that he or she is behaving in the desired way of his own free will. Once these people realize that they have tried to manipulate them, respect and sympathy could quickly flute.

- ***The Emos:*** People who act primarily from the gut, who show their feelings openly and have very strong feelings, are accordingly easier to manipulate because you just have to determine what feelings you can arouse in them in what way. Showed helplessness shows, for example, a very good effect on people with a helper complex.

- ***People are always the product of their socialization -*** the more you know about them, for example about guilt complexes, loss anxiety and these things, the better you can apply to these positions.

5. Reflect your conversation partners

This method comes from the NLP - neurolinguistic programming - and is based on the knowledge that we like it and that we are more open to the demands of others if they seem to us similar. You should not overdo it, it's not a theatrical exercise, but in moderation, you can try it by mirroring certain idiosyncrasies of your fellow human beings:

• Posture, movements, facial expressions and gestures

• Emphasized emotional attitude (cheerfulness, indifference, enthusiasm ...)

• The tone of voice, linguistic register

• Height of voice, volume, speech rate

Doing so not only improves your chances of manipulating others, but it also sharpens your powers of observation and body control.

6. Manipulation techniques that you often encounter

• Principle of reciprocity: One hand washes the other. If someone does you a favor, it may be that he is actually pursuing the goal of demanding something later on. We quickly feel committed to others and skilled people know how to take advantage of it.

• Foot-in-the-Door Technique: Also called a steady-state trap. In doing so, somebody tries to dissolve your resistance to a task or expectation by introducing you unobtrusively to the cause. Sentences such as "Look at it first" serve to make you take the first step in the desired direction.

• Herding: People tend to recognize something when other people do.

You have now learned six secrets of mind manipulation. None of them is revolutionary or mind-blowing, but combine these elements together and you get a powerful method to influence and manipulate other people's minds.

HOW TO USE DARK PSYCHOLOGY IN SEDUCTION

The 11 best techniques of seduction, according to experts

Seduction is an interesting subject in which psychology has a lot to contribute. To seduce you have to master different communication skills and different social skills, it is an act that takes place between two people.

Expectations, the image we give, the things we say and the security we show are key elements to be able to approach that person that attracts us.

Techniques and rules of seduction

Some experts, such as Robert Greene, author of the book *The Art of Seduction*, affirm that there are different techniques of seduction that practically ensure success at the time of linking (evidently not 100%).

Now, it is important to understand that each person is a world and, therefore, instead of focusing on aspects that we believe can work for everyone, it is necessary to focus on the needs of the person we want to seduce.

Seduction is an individual process in which we must analyze and intervene according to each situation. Each person has a different vision of the world and has different tastes and it is not possible to seduce all people equally.

Of course, there are a series of golden rules of seduction; are the ones you can see below.

1. Self-confidence and security

Self- confidence is not in itself a technique of seduction but an attitude, a way of showing oneself towards others.

Without self-confidence, it is impossible for the seduction process to go well. That is why first of all you have to work on the assessment that one makes of oneself and face the seduction process with a positive mentality. The security we show is crucial to captivate the person that attracts us.

If you think you have no chance with that person, you can change your mindset and downplay the issue. As I said, attitude is what matters. So do not have very high expectations (which can be frustrating), but relax and do not idealize the person you intend to seduce. Be calm and safe.

2. Be realistic

Being realistic is not a technique either, but it is a necessity. Do not pretend to use seduction techniques in situations in which failure is assured. For example, when the person is in love with their partner and is about to get married.

In some situations, seduction techniques will not be useful; However, in those that you have possibilities, follow these tips will help you break the ice and maximize your chances of knowing that person you want so much.

3. Focus on the brain

Many people make it clear that their desire is intimate with the other person, and although this is normal, it is not necessary to shout it to the four winds, especially when there is still no trust between the two.

To have options with that person, it is always better to stimulate the brain before the genitals, and that means that there is good communication and good chemistry. In other words, connect with their interests, their needs, and make them feel important.

4. Take your time

The seduction has to do with going step by step, and what makes a person want others many times in anticipation. When you find that person you are interested in, take your time. Wait a bit before getting close and start listening more than talking. Do not reveal your intention in a matter of a few minutes, since this could be unpleasant.

5. Work your social life

One of the golden rules of attraction is that no matter how much you go after someone, that is not going to make that person fall in your arms. We are usually seduced by people who socially have great value, who like other people; that is to say, that they have an active social life since in part we see their value reflected in the opinions of others.

6. Work on yourself

There is nothing more seductive than a person who is happy with what they do and is proud of themselves. That is why to please others, one must feel fulfilled and pursue their dreams. When someone connects with themselves it is easy to connect with others.

7. Detect the needs of the other person

We often think that rules or techniques for flirting work with everyone, and it is not exactly like that. Why? Because each individual is a world and has its needs. Sometimes we can hear the phrase "if you pass him or her and you'll see how you look." In reality, the only thing you can achieve with this is that it moves further away from you and the trust between you is lost.

The important thing is that the other person is fine with you, that he is well when you are around him. That's why it's better to focus on your needs instead of paying close attention to popular beliefs or generalities.

8. Generate positive feelings in the other person

And the explanation to the previous point is that people want to feel good and we want the people around us to generate positive feelings in us. These are the good times we remember because unless a person has self-esteem problems, they will tend to flee from toxic people.

9. Use the sense of humor

The best technique to flirt is to make people laugh. In

line with the previous point, there is nothing that generates more positive feelings than when we laugh with another person and have a good time, because our brain secretes neurochemicals related to pleasure and well-being: serotonin, endorphins, etc.

The sense of humor is one of the qualities of the people that attract more. This is what John Medina says, a biologist who concludes that we are attracted to people and things that are fun, interesting, intriguing and that draws our attention.

10. Create your own brand

The American newspaper The Times interviewed Arden Leigh, director of a well-known New York seduction center, and it affirms that women are more successful when they differ from other women. The seduction expert affirms that you have to think like a company, specifically with regards to branding. "Making a mark of oneself is the best way to seduce others and touch their emotional side," says Leigh.

11. The power of mystery

Think of mystery book, because you're always wanting to know more and more after each page you read. Well, the mystery is one of the most effective weapons of seduction, since it makes a person elaborate expectations of the other.

That is why it is not good to give everything at once when we want to conquer someone, but we must go step by step, letting time do its job and the other person is interested in us. These expectations and illusions, which have great seductive power, make the other person want to know more and more as we get to know each other, and the feeling intensifies over time.

7 False Myths of the Seduction Business

Maybe this does not feel too good in some sectors. I know that I might be criticized. There will even be people who will take it personally. Seem right. But I can not keep quiet about what I've proven in all this time I've been in the business.

I write this because I am tired of seeing people who, after spending hundreds or thousands of euros, remain as unhappy as the first day.

What do you want in your life?

Allow me to clarify something before anything: if all you want to read a book or pay for a seduction workshop is to sleep occasionally with women, regardless of whether the next day you will want to see again or the satisfaction that may report, then yes. Probably the business of seduction is what you are looking for.

But if what you want is to feel more valued and happy with yourself, expand and enjoy your social circle, and be able to maintain healthy sentimental relationships, then forget about that industry.

And after a few years of experience, I assure you that 9 out of 10 people in the background want the second.

What will you find in that business?

Although there are people and companies dedicated to seduction who perform an honest and very brave work, unfortunately, they are a small minority.

As a general rule, in this industry, you will find 3 types of "teachers".

1.   People with little experience who occasionally link and sell that the method they use is the method that will work for everyone.

2.   People who want fame even at the cost of their self-esteem, and record themselves doing things that border on sexual harassment.

3.   People who directly only translate or reuse content from others without contributing anything new.

The most dangerous seems to be the last ones. Without training of any kind (I do not say it is necessary to be a psychologist, but at least have a minimal idea) are dedicated to repeating concepts without even understanding them. The problem appears when what they repeat is not only not valid, it is harmful.

Beware of believing everything they tell you without putting anything to trial. Most of the gurus of seduction have not spread these myths out of evil. They have done it out of ignorance. They have simply dedicated themselves to repeating what they have read in other places because they have also believed it.

That's why I want to encourage you to be critical, to be curious, to never take anything for granted. As a sample, I leave you with 7 false refuted myths of this business selling aspirations.

1. Pretend you are until you are

That business has been selling for years that you must continually repeat that you are a fucking guy that makes women crazy (even if your life is determined to indicate otherwise). Fake it until you make it, or see what you are until you are.

Well, not only is it a lie, but it can also be harmful.

The scientific publication Psychological Science showed that positive affirmations can be very negative in people with low self-esteem. They are capable of causing precisely the opposite effect. Here is the study.

What if instead of trying to self-deceive yourself thinking that everyone is going to fall great, do you accept the fact that some people will be attracted and others will not?

Stop doing as if you were.

2. Women looking for men with "courage"

There is no doubt that they want alpha males. Men with social, economic or physical value. The more the better.

Insurance?

Can not it be that each woman looks for something in particular?

Can not it be that some reject high-value men like those who reject the umpteenth call of Movistar?

It turns out, dear friend, that showing or feigning value can also be harmful to flirt. Maybe that's not what industry gurus have told you. Beware of looking too cool because another scientific study shows that, for women seeking a stable relationship, demonstrating high social or economic value can make you attractive.

For a long time, the business of seduction has been determined to make us believe that all women are looking for the same: value. But do you want the same as the rest of the men on earth?

But for me, the problem of value goes even further. The time you spend pretending it could be time spent actually creating it. I've seen people go out with people they do not know to pretend they have more friends, people who learn magic tricks just to flirt, and even unemployed guys who say they are businessmen to sleep with women.

Maybe with some funny tricks or phrases, you can take to bed the girl who is drunk that night or wanting to walk. I doubt you will impress other types of women. In any case, when you run out of the repertoire, then what will you do?

3. All women can be seduced

There are often guys who ask "what did I do wrong with the girl at the bar who did not want to give me her phone number?" Did physical contact fail me? Did not I pass your exams correctly?

And I tell them "Why do you think you have done something wrong?"

The seduction business sells you that all women are potentially seducible, whether they have a boyfriend, a husband or even a lesbian. And they do it intentionally to keep you under constant pressure, in a world where everything comes down to linking more.

They make you believe that if a woman rejects you it's your fault. There has been a part of the seduction process that you have not done well. You must continue practicing.

Whoever wants to make you think about all that knows little about women. They can reject you for hundreds of things that have nothing to do with whether you have done well or badly, in the same way, that you do not buy all the offers they make you, no matter how good the commercials are.

4. To the divas, you must lower the fumes

One of the most widespread techniques to try to seduce attractive girls is to use ironic insults.

It's curious. Instead of recommending that you go up to their level, this business encourages you to go down to theirs. In the instrumental conditioning of psychology, this is called punishment.

And yet, it has been shown for some time in studies like this that positive reinforcement is more effective than punishment for modifying behavior. Punishment does not communicate any information about more appropriate alternative behavior and often only succeeds in substituting undesirable behavior for another. Not to mention that their results are usually temporary and bring with them several unwanted side effects, such as the girl in question associates you with negative emotions.

Check it out for yourself with two ways of saying the same thing:

• "The last time I met a girl as edge as you she ended up in my bed." Even if it's funny, you're not really telling her how you want her to behave. She can remain even more edge.

• "Ana, you look pretty funny so I think we'd laugh more if you were a little more communicative with me." First the prizes, and then you offer the possibility of a bigger prize by making it clear how you want to them behave. In this case, there is no doubt about what you want.

With this, I am not saying that there are no women who go to divas and look at you over their shoulders. But remember that it is you who has approached because you want something from her. Does that give you the right to insult her?

5. Seduction is a "game"

Being able to seduce should be a consequence of your life. The moment you consider it something separate, something detached from your real life, is when you call it a game.

If you think that seduction is something to be played, something that you have to mentalize yourself for, prepare yourself and compete, is that something is wrong in your life. If your game starts the moment you open your mouth to talk to a girl, it also ends when you let her do it.

The paradox is that to know girls, however much they

sell you infallible methods, you just have to have the guts to approach them without a rejection affecting you too much. And so that the rejection does not affect you, there is no other way than to work on your self-esteem. Which is precisely what most of the seduction industry does not do. And how they do not do it, they tell you to act as if the result does not matter.

If you continue to play you will be treating the symptoms of the problem, not the causes.

6. You can not be a 'natural'

In the slang of seduction, those men who seduce unconsciously, who have not dedicated themselves to learning how to do it, are called 'naturals'.

The reality is that a natural is no more than a person who has understood that seduction is a consequence of their way of life, while a non-natural is someone who believes that their way of living life is not seductive and then you must study how to do it.

Ask them. The kind of person they want is one who lives life according to their standards and values. It does not matter so much what you do, but how and why you do it.

Do you think that a person who only studies how to seduce them is a person who is living his life according to their principles without caring to obtain the approval of others?

And this is another of the ironies of seduction. They insist that you do not depend on the result to attract it. But how can a person who leaves behind their hobbies to learn what others want and be able to give it to them depend on the result?

If you do not care about the result, I do not know what you do studying how to attract people. I read once that "to be the man of your dreams you must become the man of your dreams" that is natural.

7. Seduction teachers have enviable lives

Absolutely. Some have lives you would never want for you. Some find it difficult to reach the end of the month, others are tired of women leaving them, and several do not even have friends because nobody supports them. Without forgetting those who dedicate themselves to this because they can not find another job.

What you see in the videos or the articles are their cases of apparent success, not the failures. They show you how they get the phone number but you do not know what happens next. And I assure you that what really happens is that many times the girls do not take calls. Did you know that many women agree to give their phone numbers only to get rid of you?

Beware who you envy. You could end up looking like him.

The consequences of this business

Instead of working from the inside out, first your relationship with yourself and then with others, the industry of seduction wants to become an obsessed person. It tells you that you can flirt up at funerals. And if you do not link, it's because you're not good enough. Continue buying books and attending workshops until you are an artist.

With all this what does he get? Well, basically people are created permanently dissatisfied and even misogynist. I'll give you 3 patterns that I'm tired of seeing:

1.   People who, despite being linked, are sad and unhappy people. They base all their happiness on the external validation of women. And when they do not have it, they suffer.

2.   People who have spent a fortune in workshops and seduction books and are still asking why the girl on Friday does not answer their calls or texts.

3.   Obsessive people who spend the entire afternoons of Sundays stopping dozens of girls on the street and

hopes to see any signs of interest.

With this book, I do not mean that learning seduction is the worst thing you could do in life. In fact, there are some good tips that can help you. I've seen guys who just needed a push to be great seducers and they've done very well. But they were already charismatic people, with clear goals and values. They just needed to perfect some details and to better themselves first.

COVERT EMOTIONAL MANIPULATION

The bonds that we build throughout our lives can encourage us to get the best out of ourselves, but they can also wear us down, threatening our emotional well-being. An example of this is the relationships affected by emotional manipulation strategies. Let's reflect on this topic.

What is emotional manipulation?

From a psychological perspective, emotional manipulation is an art that entails not only hiding bad intentions or aggressive behaviors, but also the ability to identify the emotional vulnerabilities of the other, and then implement the best strategies to manage it.

So the manipulator plays with the emotions of his victim with the sole purpose of getting away with it and that his wishes are fulfilled, establishing a covert relationship of power, being in many cases a clear act of psychological violence. Thus, the end result is that the other does not trust what he thinks, does or feels, deteriorating his image of emotional and intellectual competence.

Manipulate is knowing what to say and how to say it to favor and fulfill one's interests

However, it should be clarified that there are many types of emotional manipulation, both conscious and unconscious. From that, we can carry out each one of us when we demand that the other think or do something as we consider up to the one used by people who are in the position of victim, and the most dangerous, used by all types of abusers in a way repeated. The latter can have serious consequences on the victim's self-esteem.

Who is an emotional manipulator?

As we have seen, there are many ways to manipulate emotionally, so different profiles of manipulators are distinguished with some characteristics in common distributed among all ages, social status, sex, and culture.

The emotional manipulators are like the chameleons, camouflage artists who change their appearance depending on the environment in which they find themselves to get their victim and, therefore, their desired goal without the other people appreciating it.

They are usually very skilled people with the words capable of directing conversations towards key points that generate in the other attitudes of submission or guilt. Even many of them have a large repertoire of social skills that they will use to charm the person who will later become their victim.

This type of person also dominate non-verbal communication so sometimes only a small gesture or silence will be necessary to influence the other. But in what truly emotional manipulators have a mastery is in the detection of the Achilles heel of their victims, that is, they identify with great ease what are the weak points and vulnerabilities of the people around them.

Also, they have the constant need to feel admired and have great cravings for power and that is how they establish their relationships, exercising the role of a dominant person, although inside they are extremely insecure as affirmed by the American psychologist Susan Foward.

They are not always aware of their strategies since they usually learned from children to use the power to demand from others. A dangerous mechanism to establish links with others when used by habit because, as Voltaire said, the passion to dominate is the most terrible of all diseases of the human spirit.

How to know if we have a relationship with an emotional manipulator?

There are some warning signs that indicate that we may be immersed in a relationship with an emotional manipulator. For example, if we feel constantly pressured to do or say something we did not really want, we are afraid to express our opinion for what the other is going to think or demand without giving us an option. These types of situations usually hide big strategies of manipulation.

It is very important to stop and reflect on the relationships we are maintaining and what we feel when we are in the presence of the other. When the feelings that invade us are those related to fear, guilt, insecurity, shame or even disgust we can not let go because we can probably be manipulated.

If we are isolated, forced, devalued or not taken into account, with fear of expressing ourselves and without emotional support from the other, it is advisable that we take measures. It may also be that our way of thinking has changed or we notice that sense of identity loss because we have given ourselves completely to the wiles of the manipulator. Even, it may likely take a long time until we realize it but it is never too late.

The road to emotional autonomy

When we act under the influence of an emotional manipulator our will and way of thinking are weakened so we are not focused on our personal power. To prevent being manipulated we have to practice emotional self-defense to increase our personal resources and set limits.

For this it is important to listen to our emotions and to lose the fear of the other's anger, to be rejected and not to please others. Otherwise, we will remain immersed in the relationship between power and control established by an emotional manipulator. Having peace at any price is not the solution when we are losing ourselves.

It is convenient to take a step back and observe what is happening to be able to clarify what is wanted and begin to set limits. A good exercise is to reflect through questions such as: does it benefit me to please the other and renounce what I am? Is it necessary to please to feel loved? Am I doing what I really want or am I just letting myself go? What are my needs? The answers can be the first step to recover the power over ourselves and get out, added to a support network and even in some cases to seek professional help depending on the severity of the established link. But the important thing is to realize and start moving forward.

Let's not forget that an emotional manipulator craves the power that expresses towards the outside but forgets that as Seneca said the most powerful person is the one that is the owner of itself. So if we recover our personal power and trust and believe in ourselves, we will prevent being victims of emotional manipulation.

Eight ways to detect emotional manipulation

Emotional Manipulation is also "covert aggression".

There is no use in trying to be honest with an emotional manipulator. You make a statement and this will be given back. For example: "I am very angry because you have forgotten my birthday". Answer: "It saddens me that you think I might forget your birthday, I should have told you about the great personal stress I'm facing right now - but you'll see,...I do not want to cause you any problems, you're right, I should have left all this pain aside (Do not be surprised to see real tears at this moment) and focus on your birthday". Even when you are hearing the words you have the chilling feeling that they do not mean what they really feel it, but once they say the words you will be left with practically nothing left to say. Either that, or you will find yourself suddenly comforting them and taking care of their anguish. In any case, If you feel you are in the middle of a situation like this, do not give up! Do not get upset, do not accept your excuses that you feel like garbage. If it feels like garbage, it probably is.

Rule number 1:

If you deal with an emotional blackmailer trust your instincts, trust your senses. Once an emotional manipulator finds a maneuver that gives good results, it will be added to his list of successes and will be fed frequently with a diet based on this despicable scheme.

Rule number 2:

An emotional manipulator is the living image of a willing helper. If you ask them to do something they will always agree, and that is if they do not offer to do it first. Then, when you say "oh, thank you" they make a lot of sighs or other nonverbal signs that let you know that really, after all, they do not want to do anything of what was said. When you request it, they do not seem to want to do it, in fact, they will turn it around and try to make it seem as if they wanted to do it, and they will make you feel how irrational you are. This is a way to drive the victims crazy, a task for which the emotional manipulator is very good.

Rule number 3:

If an emotional manipulator says yes, have them account for it. Do not buy your sighs and subtleties, if they do not want to do it, have them say it straight out.

• Go crazy: They say one thing and later they assure him that they did not say it. If you are in a relationship where you begin to consider that you should keep track of everything that has been said and begin to question your own sanity, you are experiencing emotional manipulation. An emotional manipulator is an expert in turning things around, rationalizing, justifying, and describing things by turning sense. They can lie with such discretion that you can sit looking at something black and they will say it is white, and they will argue so persuasively that you will begin to doubt your own senses.

It will be very unsettling for an emotional manipulator if you start carrying a notebook and a pencil and make notes during conversations. Feel free to let them know that you are feeling very forgetful these days and that you want to record their words for posterity. The detestable thing about all this is that having to do things like these is a clear example of why you should first seriously consider moving away from them for a while. If you are loading a notebook to protect yourself, the overload indicator of the washer should be on permanently.

Rule number 4:

Guilt. Emotional manipulators are excellent traffickers of guilt. They can make you feel guilty for speaking or not speaking, for being emotional or not being enough, for giving and attending, or for not giving and not attending enough. Anything is a legitimate and open target to blame. Emotional manipulators rarely express their needs or wishes openly, they get what they want through manipulation. Guilt is not simply a way to do this, but it is a very powerful resource of manipulation. Another powerful emotion that is used is sympathy. An emotional manipulator is a great victim. They inspire a deep sense of needing support and care. The emotional manipulator rarely fights their own fights or do their own "dirty work". The crazy thing is that when you do it for them (which they never asked directly), they can turn it around and say that they certainly did not want or expected you to do anything.

Try to draw a line and not fight other people's battles or do their dirty work. A great line would be: "I have all the confidence in your ability to solve this on your own." Take a look at your answer and write down how much the debris meter measures this time.

Rule number 5:

Emotional manipulators play dirty. They do not negotiate directly. They will talk behind their backs and eventually put others in the position of telling them what they could not say to themselves. Emotional manipulators are passive aggressors, that is, they will find subtle ways to let you know that they are not happy by their side. They will tell you what they think you want to hear and then they will make a lot of mental straws to sink you. An example: "Of course I want you to go back to school, honey, you know that I support you". Then the night before the exam you are sitting at the table and your poker buddies appear, the children are crying, the volume of the TV is at maximum, and the dog needs to go out and relieve himself. All while his "little guy" is with his ass resting, staring at her.

Rule number 6:

If you have a headache an emotional manipulator will have a brain tumor! No matter what your situation, the emotional manipulator has already been there or is now, but only ten times worse. It is difficult after a while to feel emotionally connected to an emotional manipulator, as they have a detailed conversation mode and put all the attention on themselves. If you make them feel disgusted by this behavior, they will probably feel deeply hurt, or they will become very petulant and call you selfish, or they will say that you are always at the center of the scene. The point is that even though you know that this is not the case, you are left with the impossible task of proving it.

Rule number 7:

The emotional manipulator somehow has the ability to affect the emotional climate of those around him.

When an emotional manipulator is sad or angry, everyone is affected by it. He has a deep instinctive response to find some way to equalize the emotional climate of his environment with these feelings, and the quickest way to solve this situation is to make the emotional manipulator feel better by adjusting or correcting whatever is altering him. Stay with these types of losers for a long time and you will be so enmeshed and co-dependent that you will not remember that you also have needs, much less that you have the same right to satisfy them.

Rule number 8:

The emotional manipulator has no sense of responsibility. They do not take responsibility for themselves or their behavior. It's always about what everyone has done to them. One of the easiest ways to detect an emotional manipulator is that they often try to establish intimacy through the early revelation of deeply personal information that is generally of the "connect with me and feel sorry for me" type. At first, you can perceive this type of people as very sensitive, emotionally open, and perhaps somewhat vulnerable. Believe me when I tell you that an emotional manipulator is as vulnerable as a fast pitbull bully that there will always be a problem or a crisis to overcome.

HYPNOSIS

How does hypnosis work?

You have certainly heard about hypnosis, the state of waking sleep, in which the person seems totally influenced. But how does this method work? In which cases can it be used?

What is hypnosis?

Initially, hypnosis is a method developed in psychiatry. By bypassing mental processes, it theoretically makes it easier to reach the unconscious. The hypnotic state corresponds to a state of modified consciousness where things are perceived differently. This can help resurrect some childhood issues or traumas. But how does it work?

What are the different hypnosis techniques?

There are two complementary schools:

• The first, traditional is based on suggestion. The person facing the hypnotist undergoes verbal, visual and bodily injunctions. Practiced until Freud, this technique starts from the following postulate: if it is suggested to a patient to heal, he can heal. Even today, show hypnotists who have fun sleeping an entire room, belong to this school.

• The second, Ericksonian hypnosis, solicits the active participation of the patient. It is more of a state of deep relaxation, during which the patient will be able to express himself freely. The therapist uses metaphors, that is to say, a symbolic language, to guide the subject's unconscious and lead him to find the solutions to his problems.

When can one be hypnotized?

More and more used in medicine, and psychotherapy, hypnosis seems effective to fight against pain, to get rid of certain addictions or bad habits (smoking, nibbling ...), anxiety, disorders of sexuality and phobias. If the mechanisms of action are not known, and many scientists evoke the placebo effect, some hypotheses may explain the success of hypnosis:

• Pain: During the hypnotic state, the production of endorphins is at its maximum. But these are true natural painkillers, which can reduce the doses of drugs in case of back pain, migraines, etc;

• Stopping smoking: hypnosis attempts to act on psychological dependence and to substitute other behaviors. The practitioner will try to elicit the strongest suggestions, for example, the tobacco-nausea combination;

• Stress: in the first place, hypnosis, close to relaxation, rapidly decreases the impact of stressors. Then, the hypnotic state can find the appropriate threshold stimulation/excitation of good stress, so that it becomes useful again.

Is there a danger? What are the limits?

Honored with a certain mystery, hypnosis wrongly evokes a sort of occult power of the one who uses it. Do not worry, his influence on your unconscious is not all-powerful. There are securities in our brains that prevent us from doing something contrary to our values. However, be careful to choose a serious professional listed for example on the website of the French Institute of Hypnosis. This will avoid dealing with a quack.

Also, hypnosis remains a complementary method and does not replace a medical consultation. Faced with a physical or psychological problem, you must talk to a health professional who will then establish the appropriate treatment method, which hypnosis can very well be part of.

In practice

According to the French Institute of Hypnosis, the duration of a session varies between 30 and 60 minutes, and the prices are between 45 and 65 € excluding metropolises and 60 and 85 € in metropolises. If some therapists believe that the therapy ends when the goals are achieved, in practice, five to six sessions are sometimes necessary, depending on the problems to be treated.

Hypnosis surgery

Although still very mysterious, hypnosis has become, during the last ten years, a practice used in the surgical departments, as evidenced by the experience reported at the world congress of anesthesiology by Pr. Marie-Elisabeth Faymonville of the University Hospital Center of Liège. In his department, more than 4,300 patients received Hypno-sedation instead of conventional general anesthesia, mainly for plastic surgery or endocrine surgery. To explain the mechanisms involved, Pr Faymonville's team conducted various experiments that highlighted certain areas of the brain.

In light of the results, Professor Faymonville believes that "we can say that patients under hypnosis activate, in the brain, a network to better manage pain and they can significantly reduce the perception and inconvenience related to their pain. All these studies reinforce the idea that to fight against the pain, there are not only pharmaceutical strategies but also psychological strategies".

To tell the truth, hypnosis has probably existed since the beginning of mankind, according to Pr. Alain Foster of the Anesthesiology Department of the Cantonal University Hospital of Geneva (Switzerland). In medicine, the phenomenon was described for the first time in 1821 for the ablation of a breast. But it will be necessary to wait until 1955 for hypnosis to finally be officially recognized as a therapeutic method, first by the British Medical Association, then, three years later, by the American Medical Association. In anesthesia-resuscitation, hypnosis combined with a state of half-sleep and local anesthesia is now an anesthetic technique that provides comfort to patients during surgery.

Even after the operation, the use of hypnosis decreases nausea and vomiting, relieves pain and allows faster recovery.

What hypnosis is and is not.

Hypnosis is:

- A deep state of relaxation or an intense state of excitement.

- A state of increased concentration on a single thing.

- An everyday occurrence.

- An altered state of consciousness.

- A state in which the subconscious mind is more responsive (increased suggestibility).

- A state in which can be changed mental programs.

- A condition in which hypnotic phenomena can occur with appropriate suggestions.

What hypnosis is NOT...

- Sleep

- Unconsciousness

- Impotence

Hypnosis, there you are unconscious

"I think I was not hypnotized at all, I got everything."

A sentence that I keep hearing after the first hypnosis session. The many hypnotic shows on stage and television do not seem to do much to explain the phenomenon of hypnosis in the population. In particular, the assumption that hypnosis is something like unconsciousness has apparently been established in the minds of most people. I am all the more pensive about the fact that more and more people are ready to surrender to the omnipotence of a hypnotist, to lose consciousness and to wait for the things to come. But only in passing.

The fact is: hypnosis is not unconsciousness. Even in a trance, you are always fully aware of what is going on. Often you may wonder in a trance, why you have just responded in a different way or how you have come up with this unusual idea. But that's because in hypnosis, your subconscious takes over and the otherwise so dominant consciousness takes a back seat.

If not unconsciousness, then what?

Hypnosis is an altered state of consciousness in which the subconscious (the real motor and motivator of the human being) is more responsive. It needs one thing in the first place, namely rapport.

Rapport in hypnosis is the mutual relationship of trust between hypnotist and hypnotist. In other words, both have to want hypnosis, both need to agree on the goals of the session, and above all, the hypnotist must believe that the hypnotist has the necessary competence.

If these conditions are met, you will notice that a so-called leading takes place. In my therapy, this is expressed as follows:

A client tells of a car accident he suffered and then

spent two days in a coma. I urge him to tell me what happened during the two days in a coma. He replies he does not know. I say, "The coma is lifted at three, and you can tell me exactly what happened, one, two, three."

The client will respond to my request and describe all incidents. Upon my suggestion, he produced the hypnotic phenomenon of hypermnesia. That's one of the signs that I have rapport.

Where is the rapport with the stage hypnosis?

I told you what it takes for hypnosis to work:

1.   A mutual relationship of trust between the hypnotist and the hypnotist.

2.   A consensus on the objectives of the meeting.

The stage hypnotist expects that the volunteers who sign up for the hypnosis show will trust them (otherwise they'll be stupid if they sign up!) And that they agree on the goals of the session, namely:

a) experiencing something out of the ordinary,

b) overcoming one's own limitations (with the excuse that you were hypnotized and had no idea what had happened),

c) astonishing and making the audience laugh.

To be sure that they actually have the right people on

the stage, the show hypnotist will either do a couple of suggestibility tests and put the inappropriate people back in their place, or they will start the show with simple suggestions to follow and then continue with those persons who have been found particularly suggestive.

Fact is and remains: Anyone who participates in a stage show is fully conscious and knows exactly what is happening. The shows atmosphere and peer pressure make them behave as the hypnotist suggests. But of course that has its limits: If a show hypnotist would suggest that the subject runs naked on the street, then the rapport would be broken. Unless the subject has exhibitionistic traits and long wanted to have a good excuse to walk around naked on the street.

But how about in movies?

All I can say is this: forget what you've ever seen in cheap movies about hypnosis. It's just fairy tales. The fact that you hypnotize a person without their knowledge and can plant their lust for murder belongs in the field of Glupschaugen Horst Idyll (Says: Derrick) and requires no further comment.

You can not hypnotize me...

If you say that, you are right on the one hand: If you come to me with this attitude in therapy, we have no rapport and I will not be able to do much with you.

On the other hand, this saying betrays how little you understand about hypnosis. I guarantee you: Every evening, when you sit in front of the TV, fixation of the screen alone causes you to go into a light to medium trance and your subconscious mind is responsive. The only question is whether the suggestions that you get in every day do not harm your subconscious mind rather than your benefit.

Please get used to the fact that hypnosis is a natural and commonplace condition. The more you know about it, the more you can benefit from it.

Frequently Asked questions and Their Answers

Do I remember afterward?

They remember everything. Consciousness is fully present in hypnosis, but the subconscious as well. At the end of the treatment, you still know exactly what you and the hypnotherapist have said.

How am I hypnotized?

The hypnosis introduction is practiced differently. Fixing a pendulum is rather rare. Most of the time, an intense and very pleasant body journey, which you may know from autogenic training, leads to a deep state of relaxation. In the form of agreed pictures, the hypnotherapist also invites you to mental relaxation. You are complete with yourself and this condition alone is good.

And if I do not wake up again?

Hypnosis is nothing more than a very deep form of relaxation. They wake up in any case again.

Can anyone be hypnotized?

Yes. But only if you want it. The principle of voluntariness is very important.

Hypnosis works with a state of trance. Trance states are nothing out of the ordinary, they are states that occur quite naturally with each person several times a day, for example, when reading a novel and appearing inner images or when driving long distances highway. The combination of concentration and monotony naturally gives rise to such trances. It has been proven that every 45 to 90 minutes each person enters a light trance state (Ernest L. Rossi). This quite natural ability (which is even better in children) is used by the therapist to activate the inner attention.

Can I be hypnotized against my will?

No. This is not possible because a serious therapist has no interest in doing anything against the will of his clients. In addition, you only work on the topics to which you have given your consent in the preliminary discussion. In hypnosis, you know in advance exactly what the content and the goal of hypnosis will be. Incidentally, no human is infinitely influenced. Especially in hypnosis, one has healthy selfishness and only accepts what is good for oneself.

Can one remember the hypnosis afterward?

Yes, in hypnosis you are mostly only partially in a state of trance and another part stays awake and can remember everything. Those who have experience with hypnosis or meditation can also achieve deeper states of relaxation. Then one has the feeling 'to be gone without sleeping'. Incidentally, it is not necessary for the success of hypnosis to reach deeper trances. But even in this state, you keep track of what's happening.

Is hypnosis dangerous?

No. On the contrary. You can experience yourself in a state of mental and physical well-being. During hypnosis, the defense strength increases, the stress hormones are lowered, blood pressure, pulse rate, and respiratory rate drop, pain sensations diminish. In emotional experience, it can happen that dealing with problems can lead to intense feelings, as in the waking consciousness. The goal of hypnosis is to come through the problems to a successful solution. Therefore, problems should only be treated with competent therapists. In any case, it is important as with any therapy and advice, check in advance if the therapist is suitable.

Is the success of hypnosis really lasting?

The task is to change the undesirable. So the goal is an improvement. And you do not just give up improvements. The changes also persist because you make the decisions to change yourself and because the changes are in line with your own ideas and abilities.

I'm afraid of hypnosis, that's scary to me. What can you do here?

Everything unknown to us makes you curious, or it scares you. The curiosity makes us try something new, the fear makes us avoid new things. To overcome fear, one needs trust. Therefore, you should only do hypnosis with someone you trust and who respects and answers all questions. Many people worry about

143

losing control. If the fear remains, it is better to do without hypnosis.

Do you lose your will in hypnosis?

This idea of hypnosis is one of the best known.No one can be hypnotized against anything they want or their own values. Especially in hypnosis one is particularly attuned to one's own needs and one would immediately be wide awake when something happens against one's will. Hypnosis has always stimulated the imagination. If we think through this fear, and if it were really possible, then many therapists would have been able to become millionaires. They still work as normal therapists. e

In stage and show hypnosis how are people made will-less?

Stage hypnosis has nothing to do with therapeutic work. They are also more of a game with the audience. When a hypnotized person stands motionless with his eyes closed, everyone thinks he is 'gone'. Being on the stage or in the center is basically a situation in which one loses freedom. The show hypnotists skillfully choose the people who are weak and can not distinguish themselves in such situations. This is exactly what makes stage hypnosis so questionable because the"hypnotized becomes a victim and their own needs do not matter at all. The entertainment of the audience is essential.

Can I be manipulated in hypnosis?

Before the hypnosis, everything is discussed exactly between the therapist and you as a client. Your goal is also the goal of the therapist. If anything happens during hypnosis that causes you resistance, your state of relaxation slows. That means changes against your will are not possible. That would immediately lead to the end of the hypnosis.

Is hypnosis not a form of manipulation?

Hypnosis can be used to make pain controllable, to free oneself from fears, to positively influence depression, to solve problems, to remove sleep disturbances. We only know manipulation as a negative concept, meaning in the original meaning of the word 'a certain handle'. In that sense, I find the word manipulation not so bad. The pain is manipulated so that it does not hurt anymore, the fears are manipulated so that trust can develop. I've already learned well, but I still think that hypnosis does not work for me, because I can not drop myself at all. In hypnosis, you do not have to drop. Rather, it is about stepping into a state of relaxation step by step. Relaxation is also a healthy state and an experience where you can experience fearlessness. Those who can not be dropped sometimes have a longing for it. Hypnosis is a wonderful way to learn this. That you first experience yourself in control and gradually learn how you can influence that level of relaxation. Sometimes it's good to first learn autogenic training.

Do you speak during hypnosis?

As a rule, nobody speaks in hypnosis, which would prevent them from relaxing. But there is a technique in hypnosis where inner pictorial ideas are developed. Through these images, the therapist can communicate with the client and talk to him in hypnosis. The dialogue can play an important role in recognition, development, and interpretation.

I have heard that it is worse for therapy at first. Is that also the case with hypnosis?

Hypnosis is a solution-oriented method. So it is very clearly defined as a goal that can be achieved. As a result, you can get a result relatively quickly, so that you usually feel much better after hypnosis.

What does autogenic training have to do with hypnosis?

The autogenic was developed from hypnosis and is a form of self-hypnosis. There are six standardized exercises that are gradually practiced and trained. Usually, you learn one exercise a week.

What is autogenic training?

Autogenic training is one of the best-known methods of relaxation and stress management today. It is used in many health professions, in the educational field, in management, in competitive sports - ie wherever relaxation, performance, serenity and concentration are required.

And what exactly does one train during autogenic training?

The essence of autogenic training is that we do not do something actively, but that we learn to make something passive. This is about passively relaxing different body systems (muscles, blood vessels, nerves, circulation, respiration, thoughts) with the help of mental ideas. That sounds paradoxical, but we know something similar about sleep. We also can not actively create sleep, the more we strive for it, the farther away it gets.

Can anyone learn autogenic training?

Everyone can learn the autogenic training. These are very simple exercises that you learn under guidance. Then you know how to do it and you can practice the exercise at home alone.

How to learn autogenic training?

This depends on your learning type. There are courses at various educational institutions and books with exercise descriptions. Also available as an audio CD are instructions in autogenic training.

What is the difference between therapy and coaching?

The therapy is mostly about morbid conditions. Coaching is about personality development.

Can you coach yourself? There are a relatively large number of books on this subject, so what are the arguments against this?

There is nothing wrong with coaching yourself. Everyone does that too. In everything we do, we strive to make improvements. If you have enveloped or franked 100 letters, you will find that you can improve from hand to hand. So it is with everything we do: Driving, dictating letters, developing concepts. The benefit of a coach is so similar. They have also heard several topics a hundred times and have now collected methods, skills and, above all, techniques that can accelerate your personal development. The coach is a specialist in personality development. For the coach, this has the advantage that it saves time and can utilize this time more efficiently. Not only does it take longer to coach yourself, but it's also sometimes impossible to teach yourself techniques,

Where Did Hypnosis Come From, Why Use It and What To Expect

Have you tried hypnosis before? NO, then let me tell you a little about hypnosis and what you can expect to experience, just to put your mind at rest and help you get the most from this amazingly powerful form of help.

At first, there are many misunderstandings about hypnosis and I will bring up some of the most common misunderstandings. The most frequent misunderstanding is that hypnosis would be some kind of sleep. You will not sleep during the sessions. Even though the word "hypnosis" comes from the Greek word "Hypnos" which means sleep - you will not be sleeping. You may be aware of everything said during a session and that's ok because you are still in hypnosis. In some instances, you may be able to respond, and in some cases, they may wish for you to provide them with predetermined signals, or a verbal response. Yet, again, I stress that even though you may be aware of everything you say during the session, you can be assured that you are under hypnosis.

If you do completely relax and fall asleep during the session it isn't a problem. You are in a safe place and will not miss anything from the session. And there is no need to worry about not waking up. This cannot happen. Less than 10% of the population achieves such a deep trance state that they disassociate or blackout like they do when they receive anesthesia. Such people are called somnambulists and they do not consciously remember what happens during hypnosis unless the hypnotist suggests that they will. However, even these people will wake up at the end of a session. Your hearing acts like a surveillance camera, which stays alert to protect both you and your offspring. Just think of when a mother is asleep and hears her baby cry, she wakes up immediately. If someone breaks into your home while you are asleep, you will be alerted as soon as you hear a noise. Your hearing is on 24/7, taking in information and recording it. In hypnosis, they use this to your advantage, so even if you fall asleep during the session, your brain is still recording all of the information in your subconscious mind.

The history of hypnosis is fascinating but very long and detailed, so allow me to give you the basic version so you can appreciate where hypnosis came from and why hypnosis is so successful, beneficial and safe for us to use.

Hypnosis is at least more than 6,000 years old, and some say it could be older. The Ancient Egyptians, Greeks, Romans, Indians, Chinese, Persians and Sumerians all studied hypnosis and altered states of consciousness. Between the 9th and 14th centuries, a deep understanding of human psychology was achieved and therapeutic processes such as analysis, altered states of consciousness and hypnosis were used to alleviate emotional distress and suffering. This came before psychotherapy and hypnotherapy as we know them today. From the 15th and 16th centuries onwards physicians across the world developed and refined the concept of hypnosis and its uses.

In the 18th century, the most influential figure in the development of hypnosis was an Austrian physician called Dr. Frantz Anton Mesmer. Mesmer used magnets and metal frames to perform 'passes' over the patient to remove blockages (i.e.: the causes of diseases) in the magnetic forces in the body and to induce a trance-like state. Mesmer soon achieved equally successful results by passing his hands over the patient, and he named this method 'animal magnetism'. Sadly because his healing sessions were so theatrical and held in front of the public and medical practitioners, his work was ridiculed and his tangible results ignored. However, his name survived and entered our vocabulary as the verb 'mesmerise'.

Mesmer died in 1815, but a student of his named Armand de Puysegur took Mesmer's work one step further. He discovered that the spoken word and direct commands induced trance easily and noticeably faster than Mesmer's 'passes', and that a person could be operated upon without pain and anesthesia when in trance.

The earliest medically recognized record for surgery under trance was by the English Dr. James Esdaile, who performed his first operation without anesthetic in India and reached an incredible tally of 300 major operations and a thousand minor operations using hypnosis or mesmerism as it was still called at the time.

The next progression for hypnosis came from a Scottish optician named Dr. James Braid. He discovered by accident that a person focusing on an object could easily reach a trance state without the help of 'Mesmeric passes'. In 1841 he published his findings and inaccurately named his discovery 'hypnotism' based on the Greek word 'Hypnos' which means, sleep. This is a misleading name as hypnosis is not sleep, and you will remember that although you may be aware of everything I say during the session that's OK because you are still in hypnosis.

In 1891 the British Medical Association voted in favor of the use of hypnosis in medicine but it was not approved until 1955, 64 years later! It was then that The American Medical Association took notice of a patient that underwent a Thyroidectomy, or the surgical removal of the thyroid, without anesthesia. The only aid for pain reduction was hypnosis. As demonstrated in the thyroid surgery, blocking pain is one of the effective and practical uses for hypnosis. Weight control, cigarette smoking addiction, motivation to exercise, improving study habits, controlling nervous habits, and developing healthy self-esteem are but a few of the conditions that can be influenced, with positive results, through therapeutic hypnosis.

Now let me put some of your possible concerns to rest and to remove some questions you may have from your mind.

Hypnosis can only occur if you want it to. You can only be hypnotized if you allow it. I cannot just approach you and hypnotize you without you knowing about it allowing it. This means that hypnosis is safe for everyone that wants to use it to help with and more!

Hypnosis is not some form of mystical mind control that robs you of your will or ability to make informed choices. Hypnosis is an altered state of awareness, that makes you more susceptible to suggestions and directions that are intended to assist you in making positive behavioral and physical changes in things like weight control, cigarette smoking addiction, motivation to exercise, improving study habits, controlling nervous habits and developing healthy self-esteem. It is just one of many methods of therapy that can help in a wide variety of ways, for a vast number of behavioral and physical problems.

Hypnosis is not a form of mind control. You are

always in control. If I make an unwelcome, inappropriate or destructive suggestion, your mind will reject it and you will become fully alert. Under hypnosis, you cannot be forced into doing anything against your will or your moral code. If anything happens during the session that needs your immediate attention you will still be able to deal with it. Just count "one-two-three" mentally and you'll be fully awake, or simply just open your eyes.

During your hypnosis session, you may not think that you are in a trance, but you will be able to sense your focus narrow and your breathing slow as you begin to relax and enter the Alpha state. Alpha is a level of consciousness or a trance, which is one level below being wide-awake or fully conscious, known as the Beta state of consciousness. In the Alpha state, you may become up to two hundred times more susceptible to suggestion and direction as a person in full consciousness, or the Beta state.

To describe the benefits of the Alpha state, imagine there is a pipeline going directly through the conscious into the subconscious mind. I then 'drop' the seeds of suggestion, which you have asked me to plant & help you with, into this pipe. In the subconscious, these suggestions are 200 times more likely to be effective than the things we tell ourselves in our normal Beta state. This is because they reorganize our roots of thought and behavior. They change our perception for the better. Hypnotic suggestions give people more control over subconscious mental frameworks which otherwise might debilitate their lives indefinitely. Hypnosis is a way to reorder the mind's associations into a more healthy and positive direction.

Once the suggestions and associations are in place, the therapist makes sure nothing else will be able to disassociate them in the future. When a problem is solved, it is usually solved for good. For example, most weight control cases can be treated symptomatically. It would take 1-6 sessions, or about 21 days to form and own new habits. Sometimes with weight control, we have to delve a little deeper to find the root cause of the weight gain, and this could take additional sessions, but the results at the end will justify investing this extra time. An American Health Magazine study found that psychoanalysis gave a 38% recovery after 600 sessions, behavior therapy gave a 72% recovery after 22 sessions, and hypnosis gave an amazing 93% recovery after 6 sessions. As you can see, hypnosis has been proven to safe and very effective at helping you reach your goals quickly.

Hypnosis is a completely normal state, it's something that you experiences every day. For example, when you are absorbed by a great movie or a TV-show then you are in a state of hypnosis. If you've ever been driving to work or to the store and you wondered how you got there because your mind was thinking about a thousand other things, you've experienced hypnosis. If you've ever been in the zone where you are totally focused on the task at hand and nothing else, you've been in hypnosis. If you've ever found yourself day-dreaming, you were in hypnosis. Even when you are reading a good book you can be so absorbed that you don't hear when someone talks to you. Your brain is then in a different state - hypnosis. But it isn't necessary to do things like watch movies or reading good books. It can also be boring stuff, which puts you in a hypnotic state, as an unexciting lecture. When someone talks with a monotonous voice it can be difficult to stay focused. Maybe you begin to dream about something more exciting - that is also hypnosis.

Just remember that you may be aware of everything I say during the session and that's ok because you are still in hypnosis, you can always bring yourself back to the waking Beta state by opening your eyes or counting "One-two-three" in your mind, and above all, you are always in control.

Why Does Self Hypnosis Work and How Is It Different From Stage Hypnotism?

When you are faced with what seems an insurmountable problem, you are willing to try even unconventional means. When all your sincere attempts to change your bad habits, whether smoking or overeating fail, it is time to look at another way. It is time to recognize that all the pills, dieting, and exercise will not help you if something always seems to sabotage your efforts. If the issue lies within your subconscious, it is time to consider self-hypnosis.

Self Hypnosis versus Stage Hypnosis

There are several misconceptions about self-hypnosis. Sometimes, people confuse it with stage hypnosis, it is not the same as stage hypnosis. The latter is, obviously, performed on stage for the entertainment of an audience. Self-hypnosis is done in a safe and secure environment of your own home. Stage hypnosis relies frequently on two methods: deceiving the volunteer and the audience, and illusion. Self-hypnosis focuses on helping the individual realize their reality.

While both works with the individual in a trance-like state, the rationale behind them differs entirely. A stage hypnotist is seeking to impress the audience; you, as your own hypnotist, are trying to correct old habits, retrain your subconscious and start to live the life as it is meant to be lived. In essence, the two differ on very many levels. From the absence of a stage to accomplishing a useful purpose, stage hypnosis is very different from self-hypnosis. Only some of the techniques used are the same.

What is Self Hypnosis?

If self-hypnosis is not stage hypnosis, what is it? The answer is both simple and complex. Self-hypnosis is an altered state of consciousness. It is a trance-like state you guide yourself to attain. It is truly a mind-shifting approach to the realization of a goal. It is working with your own mind to create a new reality with the purpose of change in your mind.

What does it do?

In reaching down deep into your subconscious, you work to create certain changes which will ultimately result in changes in your life. You harness your subconscious to your mindful self to accomplish a specific goal or realize a change in your life. You can use self-hypnosis for:

- Simple relaxation

- To gain control overeating and therefore, restore and maintain a healthy diet and lifestyle

- To quit smoking

- To improve your own self-image

- To triumph over certain fears or phobias in your

life - some may prevent you from accomplishing what you wish to do

• To improve your ability to remember things and people

Self Hypnosis - the Advantages

Self-hypnosis has many purposes. Basically, however, this technique intends to help you pursue your dream, to guide you to retrain your subconscious to transform your life. Self-hypnosis lets you shift the thought processes locked in your subconscious so you can stop smoking, never overeat and get rid of those fears that haunt you.

This is an advantage over many traditional approaches. Retraining your subconscious to accept your goals is more beneficial and healthy than popping pills. This is one of the best advantages of self-hypnosis, yet, there are many others. Among them you will find the following:

• The ability to learn how to perform the skill of self-hypnosis is relatively easy

• The overall cost is far less than many other types of self-help instruction and certainly far less expensive than therapy sessions. All you require are a few books and instructional tapes or downloads for MP3 player or iPod.

• You can perform it on your own time. There is no

need to worry about making and keeping appointments.

• You can perform self-hypnosis in your own space. You can select a safe, secure and quiet space in your own home.

• If you go to a cottage or away for the weekend, you can bring your tools with you. It, therefore, allows you to continue to reinforce your goals without missing a beat. In fact, when you master the skill, you can use self-hypnosis almost anywhere successfully.

Self-hypnosis can help you with the solutions to many of your problems. It is not a quick-fix. It works with you to help you find the answer. Self-hypnosis requires time, energy and effort.

CONCLUSION

The Power of Your Mind is Within Your Control

The human mind is a very complex matter and it takes many years for one to comprehend its intricacies and scientists are still in pursuit of it.

Today, many mind control techniques and devices have evolved and designed and every one has its own merits and demerits. Mind control is a relatively neutral concept that involves an attempt to communicate with one's own mind. This, in effect, helps to find out the ways and means of dealing with and use the abilities to the maximum level.

In fact, the power of the mind is so great that we do not sense its existence unless and until it gives out any negative effect. Then, it becomes essential to learn to control the mind. But if sensed earlier, it would be very helpful to lead a better life. There are many techniques to learn mind control such as hypnosis, subliminal techniques, silent treatment and so on.

The power of mind control is such that it creates a big revolution in the inner self and those around. It helps to tap the resources of the mind and synchronize with the thoughts. Controlling the mind has benefits like building a good and solid relationship and prospering in life. When the mind is controlled properly, in the right way, the conscious and subconscious brain will get enhanced.

The first step towards learning to control the mind is to realize that the thoughts are the most motivating factor and affect the mind and thus, controlling the mind primarily involves controlling the thoughts. Also, it is necessary to learn how the mind operates in order to learn to control the mind and with the techniques learned in this book will help a long way in achieving learning to control the mind.